OPEN HOUSE
IN NEW ENGLAND

THE HARRISON GRAY OTIS HOUSE (1795) BOSTON

OpenHouse

IN NEW ENGLAND

by

SAMUEL CHAMBERLAIN

WITH 280 PHOTOGRAPHS
BY THE AUTHOR

BONANZA BOOKS · NEW YORK

This edition published by Bonanza Books,
a division of Crown Publishers, Inc., by
arrangement with Hastings House, Publishers, Inc.

(D)

Printed in the United States of America

Open House in New England

Parson Capen House, Topsfield, Mass.

Table of Contents

Open House in New England

Rebecca Nurse House, Danvers, Mass.

I

Introduction

Words can tell the history of early New England, from its first epochal days at Plymouth to the proud moment when it emerged from the Revolution, a vital part of a brave young Republic. But the story can be related more eloquently by historians which are mute and wordless—its surviving landmarks. Old houses and taverns are inextricably tied up with the life and drama of Colonial days. The lives of our ancestors, the personalities of our noted men of history and of literature, are revealed by their homes, quite as much as by their writings.

It is a matter of extraordinary interest, therefore, to know that over two hundred of New England's old houses not only remain standing, but are open to the public, and are usually furnished, restored and richly endowed with historic relics. This fact gives the present volume a three-fold opportunity: to outline the architectural romance of the old houses; to sketch briefly the historic facts which make them interesting; and to serve as a reliable pictorial guide for those who desire to visit them. The architectural biography may well come at the outset, since it provides a compact picture of the whole theme.

Only at the dawn of Colonial New England did the Pilgrims and the earliest pioneers content themselves with crude shelters. Their first edifice in the new land was a fireplace, onto which they attached a crude one-room dwelling with a garret and a steep roof. If more room became needed, a similar structure was added to the other side of the fireplace. Upon the heels of these first pioneers came hardy settlers from England, many good craftsmen being in their number. They were intent upon building permanent dwellings and at first, instead of developing the rude shacks of their predecessors, they erected traditional wooden manor houses, precisely as they had done at home. These had ornamental overhangs, steep roofs and leaded casements, and were almost medieval in character. They did not prove entirely adapted to the new conditions, which included hostile Indians, different raw materials and a more rigorous climate. A more local style soon evolved. Its most common expression was a house of four rooms, two upstairs and two down, all clustered about a huge central chimney of stone or brick. Between the lower rooms was a narrow entrance hall and a stairway clinging to the chimney. The floors of the upper rooms were held up by a huge beam, called the "summer," which was supported by the chimney masonry and the outside wall. The foundation of the house was often composed of mere field stones, laid without mortar. Upon these was placed a massive timber, or sill, which served as a base for the sturdy oak frame. The house almost always faced South.

As the early Colonial family grew to sizable proportions, wings and ells were built on, providing additional shelter. A "lean-to" was added, carrying the rear roof closer to the ground, and providing more rooms. Thus the "salt-box" type was created. At first the "lean-to" was an added wing, an afterthought after marriage, so to speak, but later it became a built-in feature of new houses. The interiors were dominated by the huge fireplace, and were far from unattractive. The large beams and other timbers were skillfully fastened together, tongued and pinned and often decorated with moldings and chamfers. The partitions usually consisted of wide vertical planks, molded at the edges. Woodwork was left unpainted, to darken with age. A few houses of the time were built, not around a central chimney, but between two massive ends of stone or brick.

As peace and prosperity came to the Colonists, their homes took on more amplitude and distinction. New houses were built with four and five rooms on each floor, instead of two. The single great central chimney became supplanted by two others, each heating two rooms, upstairs and down. Between them ran a spacious central hall, providing good circulation for the first time. In plan these new larger houses were really a pair of two-room houses of the early period, turned sideways and separated by a wide hallway. The house became more nearly square, and since a flat gable looked none too well, gambrel and hipped roofs were devised to cover the increased span. The leaded window panes gave way to double hung sashes with small wooden muntins. More attention was given to fine carpentry, good panelling and doorways, and a pronounced Georgian character crept into the wealthier houses. Walls were plastered now, and ceiling beams were concealed. More wings and ells were added as the family continued to grow.

After the architectural lull of the Revolution, a new sophistication began to seep in from Europe. Our carpenters and woodworkers studied books of measured drawings from England, and the delicate influence of Sir Christopher Wren, well known even before the Revolution, and the Brothers Adam began to be felt in the new Republic. The central-hall plan led to better balanced houses, more formal and imposing. Ceiling heights lifted and entrance doorways became more pretentious, embracing transoms and sidelights. The use of panelling became less common, and the cameo-like Adam mantelpiece appeared. The three-story mansion arrived impressively, its best expression being in the exquisite and dignified designs of Charles Bulfinch and Samuel McIntire, the carver-architect of Salem. From this praiseworthy peak, American domestic architecture disintegrated by degrees, pausing in the process to indulge in an interesting interlude of Neo-Classic impulse. In the early 19th century the house was frequently placed at right angles to its former position, so that the gable end faced the street. This permitted the use of an impressive portico with the gable forming the pediment. A result of this juxtaposition was a new interior plan which, however, never became standardized. The decadence of house design became increasingly evident, ending in a complete débacle in the late 19th Century. During this time our old houses were looked upon with indifference, if not with scorn, and many splendid examples were torn down. The pendulum of appreciation began to swing back during the first years of the 20th Century. Old houses were rescued from oblivion, restored, and often thrown open to the public as "house museums." At present a definitely improved taste in contemporary home building is evident. The "machine to live in" has made its appearance, but appears to be coolly received in New England. Here, in condensed form, are the essentials of the story.

Fortunately these essentials can be emphasized by more eloquent narrators, the old houses themselves. The recent revival in interest has meant that scores of old houses have been reclaimed and restored to their original state within the last few decades. In the ensemble they reveal not a text-book recital of the drama of Colonial days but a stirring, intimate and graphic picture, which could be achieved in no other way. Taking as examples *only* those old houses which are now open to the public (and the later chapters could also be written quite as well by houses which are hermetically sealed to the public gaze), it is possible to follow the story of the New England house step by step, and to find abundant illustration for each of the transitions outlined above. From the earliest, steep-roofed English types, more Gothic than "Colonial," through the primitive farmhouse, the more ample residence of pre-Revolutionary days, to the opulent mansions of the great merchant and shipping era, the sequence runs without interruption. The illustrations which form the main portion of this book have been arranged *approximately* in that chronological order, so that the sweep of events, both architectural and historical, may unfold itself naturally. I stress the word "approximately" because there is no more uncertain factor in this entire study of old houses than the *precise* date of construction. Often it cannot be determined with accuracy. Experts, owners and archaeologists frequently disagree among themselves on the date of a house. According to one recognized authority, no old New England house before 1651 possesses *documentary* proof of its age. The dates used to determine the chronology of these photographs have been accepted without question from the best available sources, but, in the case of the earlier dates in particular, they are *not submitted as authoritative.*

The balance of this volume is divided into four chapters, the first of which should prove the most useful. This contains a carefully revised and edited post-war list of old New England houses which are open to the public at certain times of the years. It is intended to serve as a reliable guide to visitors interested in old houses, their furnishings and their history. The second chapter is devoted to a photographic panorama of Seventeenth Century houses in New England, accompanied by a brief descriptive text. The houses are presented chronologically from 1630 to 1699, regardless of their location. The third and fourth chapters deal with houses built in the Eighteenth and Nineteenth Centuries, thus providing a continuous study of the development of the New England house from the primitive beginnings up to the brink of the abyss of ghastly taste which developed in the 1840's. Finally there is an index, listing the houses alphabetically. Thus the houses are listed by location, by date and by the hazards of the alphabet. Not all of the "open houses" are illustrated. For geographical reasons, or because of bad luck in photographing weather, some of them have not been pictured in this edition. However, the author cherishes the fond hope of visiting and photographing these few exceptions before the next edition of this book appears. It is hoped that the present pageant of photographs will throw some light upon the incomparable heritage of historic houses which is one of New England's most cherished possessions.

Open House in New England

Pardee-Morris House, New Haven, Conn.

II

A List of Old New England Houses Which are Open to the Public

NOTE: Although a great deal of research and editorial care have gone into the compilation of this list, the author makes no claim that it is entirely complete. Without question there are other houses which should be included and will be, in future editions of this book. The present and fifth edition contains over fifty houses not previously listed. If houses of pronounced architectural or historical interest are open to the public, and are omitted from this list, the author would welcome words of enlightenment.

Every care has been taken to give complete and accurate information about these particular houses, 242 in number, so that the list, as far as it goes, will have practical value. Questionnaires were sent during 1946, 1947 and 1948 to the owners of each old house, who responded very generously and supplied most of the data here presented. Only information based upon such positive sources has been used, and thus, it is hoped, a minimum of errors will appear. The matter of dates is always open to controversy, and the author begs the privilege of disclaiming responsibility for them. This list does not constitute a guarantee that *all* of the houses will be open at the hours mentioned, or at the admission fee indicated. Changes are constantly taking place, some houses returning to private occupancy while others are newly opened to visitors. But these cases are a small minority. In case of uncertainty about a house being "open" or not, it is advisable to precede your visit by a written inquiry or a telephone call. The odds are overwhelmingly in favor of a prompt and cordial response in the affirmative. Readers will undoubtedly find, as did the author, that the custodians of these old houses are gracious and helpful practitioners of the art of true New England hospitality.

This list is alphabetical by states: Connecticut, Maine, Massachusetts, New Hampshire, Rhode Island and Vermont. The towns in each state are listed alphabetically. The identical information about each house is given as briefly as possible: correct name, street address, date, original builder, present owner, hours open to the public, exhibits and admission fees, if any. No attempt has been made to evaluate and, needless to say no outside influence has entered into the selections on the list. Its sole aim is to be of impartial assistance to visitors to the old houses.

NOTE: All admission prices and data are naturally subject to change. In most cases, the admission fees are now slightly higher than they appear in this list.

CONNECTICUT

ANSONIA
RICHARD MANSFIELD HOUSE, (Page 163), 35 Jewett St. Built 1747-1748. Owned by the Antiquarian and Landmark Society, Inc. of Connecticut. Occupied by Reverend Richard Mansfield, first Episcopal rector of Derby.

CLINTON
JOHN A. STANTON MEMORIAL, (Page 202), 63 East Main St., near Congregational Church Green. Built 1789 by Adam Stanton. Owned and operated by the Hartford National Bank & Trust Company, Trustee. OPEN: week days 2 to 5, the year round. Closed Sundays. EXHIBITS: Post-Revolutionary country store, Governor Buckingham's room, Court cupboard, Abraham Pierson well, old French wall papers, costumes, etc. No admission fee.

EAST LYME
THOMAS LEE HOUSE, (Page 81), Boston Shore Road, (Route 56). Built about 1660 by Thomas Lee. Restored 1914. Owned and operated by the East Lyme Historical Society. OPEN: year round by appointment. EXHIBITS: old pewter, china, kitchen equipment, etc. ADMISSION: 25 cents, children under twelve free.

FARMINGTON
STANLEY-WHITMAN HOUSE, (Page 82), 37 High Street. Built about 1660. Restored 1934. Owned and operated by The Village Green and Library Association. OPEN: Tuesdays, Wednesdays, Fridays and Saturdays 10 to 12, 2 to 5, Fridays and Saturdays only during the winter. Closed Sundays. EXHIBITS: old china, glass, silver, pewter, documents and furnishings of the period. Also an herb garden. ADMISSION: 30 cents, children 9 cents.

GREENWICH
PUTNAM COTTAGE, (Page 155), 243 East Putnam Ave. (Post Road). Built 1731. Originally Knapp's Tavern. Owned by Israel Putnam Association. Operated by the Putnam Hill Chapter, Daughters of the American Revolution. OPEN: Monday, Thursday, Friday and Saturday, 10 to 5, the year round. Closed Sundays.

GUILFORD
HYLAND HOUSE, (Page 80), Boston St. Built about 1660 by George Hyland. Rear addition built 1720. Owned and operated by Dorothy Whitfield Historical Society. OPEN: week days 11 to 4, from mid-June to October. Closed Sundays. Furnished with pieces of the period. ADMISSION: 25 cents, children under 12 free.

GUILFORD   HENRY WHITFIELD HOUSE, (Page 63), Whitfield St. Built 1639 by Reverend Henry Whitfield. Restored 1868, and in 1936, to its original pattern. Owned by the State of Connecticut and operated by a Board of Trustees. OPEN: daily except Mondays 10 to 5, April through October, 10 to 4, December through March. Closed in November. EXHIBITS: rare specimens of Colonial furniture and relics. This is the oldest stone house in New England, perhaps in the country. No admission fee.

LEBANON   GOVERNOR JONATHAN TRUMBULL HOUSE, Lebanon Center on the Green. Built 1740 by Joseph Trumbull, father of Jonathan. Remodeled 1935. Owned and operated by the Daughters of the American Revolution, State of Connecticut. OPEN: Tuesday, Thursday and Saturday, 10 to 5, May 1 to November 1. EXHIBITS: Original Trumbull Colonial furnishings. Attractive gardens. ADMISSION: 25 cents, children under twelve free.

LITCHFIELD   TAPPING REEVE HOUSE, (Page 191), South St. Built 1773 by Judge Tapping Reeve. Restored 1930. Owned and operated by the Litchfield Historical Society. OPEN: week days 10 to 12, 2 to 5, from June 1 to November 1. Sundays 2 to 5. EXHIBITS: Colonial furniture, manuscripts and records of law students, collection of books belonging to Judge Reeve. Old fashioned style formal garden. Here was founded the first law school in America. ADMISSION: 30 cents, children under 12, tax only of 5 cents.

MADISON   NATHANIEL ALLIS HOUSE, (Page 159), Boston St. (Route 1). Built 1739 by Nathaniel Allis. Owned and operated by the Madison Historical Society. OPEN: week days 2 to 6, June to October. Closed Sundays. Furnished as old-time residence. ADMISSION: 25 cents.

MILFORD   EELS-STOWE HOUSE, (Page 88), 34 High St. Built 1669 by Colonel Samuel Eels. Restored 1930. Owned and operated by the Milford Historical Society. OPEN: certain week days. No admission fee.

NEW HAVEN   BOWDITCH HOUSE, 275 Orange St. Built about 1800 by David Hoadley. Owned by Emerson L. Munson and operated as the Munson Gallery. OPEN: all year, Monday through Saturday, 8:30 to 5. Saturday 8:30 to 12:30. Art Exhibits at regular intervals. Eli Whitney was living in this house at the time of his death. No admission fee.

NEW HAVEN   PARDEE-MORRIS HOUSE, (Page 97), 325 Lighthouse Road, Morris Cove, East Haven side. Original part built about 1680-85 by Eleazer Morris. Wing added 1767. Burned by the British 1779 and rebuilt the same year. Owned and operated by the New Haven Colony Historical Society. OPEN: week days except Mondays 10 to 5, Sundays 2 to 5, from May 1 to November 1. EXHIBITS: early American furnishings and an old-time herb garden. No admission fee.

NEW LONDON   HEMPSTEAD HOUSE, 11 Hempstead St. Built about 1678, with subsequent additions. Owned and maintained by the Antiquarian & Landmarks Society, Inc. of Connecticut.

NEW LONDON   HUGUENOT HOUSE, (Page 165), Truman St. Built about 1751 by Nathaniel Hempstead. Now a tea room.

NEW LONDON   SHAW MANSION, (Page 170), 11 Blinman St. Built 1756 by Captain Nathaniel Shaw. Owned and operated by the New London County Historical Society. OPEN: week days 10 to 12, 2 to 5, the year round. Closed Sundays. EXHIBITS: portraits, china, antiques, whaling relics, and the room where Washington slept. ADMISSION: 25 cents, children 10 cents.

OLD LYME THE FLORENCE GRISWOLD HOUSE, Main St. (Route 1), next to the Lyme Art Gallery. Built 1817 by William Noyes. Samuel Belcher, architect. Owned and operated by the Florence Griswold Association, Inc. OPEN: daily, except Monday, 2 to 5, June through August. EXHIBITS: painted panels, furnishings of the period, portrait of Florence Griswold. "Here in 1900 first foregathered the men who founded the nucleus of America's first Summer Art Group, now the Lyme Art Association." ADMISSION: 25 cents.

SOUTH COVENTRY NATHAN HALE HOMESTEAD. Birthplace of Nathan Hale, built by Deacon Hale, his father. This shrine is to be administered by the Antiquarian & Landmarks Society, Inc. of Connecticut.

STRATFORD JUDSON HOUSE, (Pages 150, 151), 967 Academy Road. Built 1723 by David Judson. Restored 1885. Owned and operated by the Stratford Historical Society. OPEN: Fridays and Saturdays 2 to 5:30, May to October, and by appointment. A typical New England home, fine interiors, slave quarters, etc. ADMISSION: 25 cents, children under 12 free.

WALLINGFORD HISTORICAL HOUSE, (Page 189), 180 South Main St. Built 1770. Owned and operated by the Wallingford Historical Society. OPEN: week days 9 to 5, Sundays 2 to 5, the year round. EXHIBITS: documents, pictures and relics of historic interest. No admission fee.

WALLINGFORD NEHEMIAH ROYCE HOUSE, 538 North Main St. Built in 1672 by Nehemiah Royce and restored by Lucy Atwater Royce in 1924. Owned and operated by the Society for the Preservation of New England Antiquities. Miss Helen E. Royce, custodian. OPEN: week days 9 to 11, 3 to 5, during July and August. EXHIBITS: 17th Century furniture, Currier and Ives print, pewter, china, painted tin-ware, wooden-ware, costumes, quilts, rare panelling, Staffordshire figures, etc. ADMISSION: 25 cents.

WETHERSFIELD WEBB HOUSE, (Page 166), 211 Main St. Early portion built 1678. Front portion built 1752 by Joseph Webb. Restored 1916. Owned and operated by The Connecticut Society of the Colonial Dames of America. OPEN: week days 10 to 5, the year round. Sundays 1 to 5. EXHIBITS: antique furniture, old china, fine woodwork. In this house General Washington planned the siege of Yorktown with General Rochambeau. ADMISSION: 25 cents, children 10 cents.

WINDSOR ELLSWORTH HOMESTEAD, (Page 160), 778 Palisado Ave., (Route 5A), between Windsor and Windsor Locks. Built 1740 by David Ellsworth. Owned and operated by the Connecticut Daughters of the American Revolution. OPEN: daily except Wednesdays, 10 to 5, Sundays 1 to 5, from May to December. EXHIBITS: fine Colonial pieces, heirlooms, etc. Presidents Washington and Adams visited Ellsworth here during their terms of office. ADMISSION: 25 cents, children 10 cents.

WINDSOR WALTER FYLER HOUSE, (Page 62), 96 Palisado Ave. Built 1640 by Lieutenant Walter Fyler. Four rooms added about 1765. Owned and operated by the Windsor Historical Society. OPEN: by appointment. No admission fee.

WINSTED SOLOMON ROCKWELL HOUSE, (Page 237), 225 Prospect St. Built 1813 by Solomon Rockwell. Owned and operated by the Winchester Historical Society. OPEN: week days except Monday 2 to 5, from June 15 to October 1. Closed Sundays. EXHIBITS: furniture, portraits, woodwork. No admission fee.

WOODBURY GLEBE HOUSE, (Page 114), Hollow Road, just west of Main St. Built about 1690. Remodelled 1740. Owned by the Diocese of Connecticut. Operated by Seabury Society for the Preservation of Glebe House. OPEN: week days 10 to 5, the year round. Sundays 1 to 5. EXHIBITS: early American pieces, original panelling, a secret door, documents and pictures. Voluntary contributions.

MAINE

AUGUSTA
THE BLAINE MANSION, (Page 243), 192 State St. Built 1830-36 by Captain James Hall. Owned by the State of Maine. This is the Executive Mansion, occupied by the Governor and his family. Formerly the home of James G. Blaine, presidential nominee. OPEN: by appointment.

AUGUSTA
FORT WESTERN (Page 169), Bowman St., bordering the Kennebec River. Built in 1754. OPEN: daily during the summer months. EXHIBITS: two restored block houses and the original garrison house, restored and furnished with Colonial antiques.

AUGUSTA
REUEL WILLIAMS HOUSE, 74 Cony St. Built in 1797 by Colonel Arthur Lithgow. Remodeled in 1806 by Reuel Williams. Owned by Mrs. William Allen Smith and Mr. Henry King Smith. The house contains French hand blocked wall paper, depicting Captain Cook's voyages, in an octagonal room, installed in 1806. The house will be shown to anyone who is genuinely interested.

BRUNSWICK
HARRIET BEECHER STOWE HOUSE, 63 Federal St. Built in 1804 by Parson Titcomb. Remodeled 1946 as an inn. Owned by Mary Baxter White. Operated by Mary Baxter White and Elizabeth R. Kochs. OPEN: the year round, at reasonable hours. Harriet Beecher Stowe wrote "Uncle Tom's Cabin" while residing here (1850-1852). The house is furnished with antiques. A gift shop is in the adjoining barn. No admission fee.

CASTINE
BLAKE HOUSE, corner Main and Court Sts. Built in 1797 by Parson Mason. Wing added in 1857. Owned by Mrs. Lillian Blake. Operated by Sarita Blake Porter. OPEN: the year round. Some of the original furnishings still remain. No admission fee.

COLUMBIA FALLS
RUGGLES HOUSE (Page 233), Main St. Built 1810 by Aaron Simmons Sherman for Judge Thomas Ruggles. Owned and operated by an Incorporated Society. OPEN: daily, upon application. EXHIBITS: remarkable interior woodwork. Voluntary contributions.

ELLSWORTH
BLACK HOUSE, (Page 239), Surry Road, (Route 15), from Ellsworth. Built in early 19th Century by Colonel John Black. Owned and operated by the Hancock County Trustees of Public Reservations. OPEN: week days and Sundays during daylight hours, May 30 to October 31. Other times by appointment. EXHIBITS: furnishings of the period. ADMISSION: 50 cents.

FARMINGTON
NORDICA HOMESTEAD, 2¼ miles north of Farmington village, on the Rangeley Road. Built about 1840. Restored 1928. Owned and operated by the Nordica Memorial Association. OPEN: week days and Sundays, early morning until 7 p.m., evenings by appointment, May to November. EXHIBITS: four rooms devoted to Lillian Nordica's possessions, operatic costumes, opera scores, portraits, furniture, china, glass, etc. ADMISSION: 25 cents, children under 12, 10 cents.

GORHAM
BAXTER MUSEUM, (Page 221), 63 South St. Built about 1798 by Isaac Gilkey. Restored 1907. Owned by the Town of Gorham. Operated by the Baxter Museum Committee. OPEN: Wednesdays and Saturdays 2:30 to 5, July and August. Closed Sundays. EXHIBITS: relics of the town's history. ADMISSION: 10 cents.

KITTERY POINT
LADY PEPPERRELL HOUSE, (Page 176). Built about 1760. Owned and operated by the Society for the Preservation of New England Antiquities. Oscar T. Clark, custodian. OPEN: expected to be open week days during summer months. EXHIBITS: fine period furniture and furnishings. ADMISSION: 50 cents.

MACHIAS

BURNHAM TAVERN, (Page 189), corner Main and Free Sts. Built 1770 by Job Burnham. Restored 1907. Owned and operated by the Hannah Weston Chapter, Daughters of the American Revolution. OPEN: Saturdays 2 to 5, June to October, and by appointment. Closed Sundays. EXHIBITS: relics of the Revolution. ADMISSION: 10 cents.

NAPLES

THE MANOR, (Page 208), on Route 302. Built about 1799 by Dr. George Peirce and remodeled in 1929. Owned and operated by Greta M. Mendelsohn as a summer inn. OPEN: June to October.

NORTH EDGECOMB

FORT EDGECOMB (Page 232), off Route 27, well marked by signs. Built 1808-1809. OPEN: during the summer months. An old wooden fort, containing fine timber work.

PORTLAND

LONGFELLOW BIRTHPLACE, (Page 198), 161 Fore St., corner Hancock St. Built 1784 by Captain Stephenson, uncle of the poet. Owned and operated by the International Longfellow Society. OPEN: week days and Sundays, 8 to 6, June to October. EXHIBITS: memorabilia of Henry Wadsworth Longfellow. ADMISSION: Single 50 cents, 2 or more visitors, 25 cents each.

PORTLAND

L. D. M. SWEAT MANSION, (Page 222), 103 Spring St., (entrance through Sweat Memorial). Built 1800 by Hugh McClellan, Alexander Parris, architect. Owned and operated by the Portland Society of Art. OPEN: week days except Monday, 10 to 4:30, the year round. Sundays 2 to 4:30, during winter months only. EXHIBITS: fine hall and staircase. No admission fee.

PORTLAND

WADSWORTH-LONGFELLOW HOUSE, (Page 199), 487 Congress St. Built 1785-86 by General Peleg Wadsworth. Third story added 1815. Owned and operated by the Maine Historical Society. OPEN: week days 9:30 to 5, June 15 to September 15. Closed Sundays. EXHIBITS: possessions of Wadsworth and Longfellow families, formal garden, etc. ADMISSION: 30 cents.

SOUTH BERWICK

CAPTAIN JEWETT HOUSE (Sarah Orne Jewett Memorial), (Page 192), 101 Portland St. Built 1774 by John Haggins. Owned and operated by the Society for the Preservation of New England Antiquities. Mrs. Georgia A. Tapley, custodian. OPEN: week days 9 to 5, during summer months. Sundays by appointment. EXHIBITS: fine interior, furnished with antiques. ADMISSION: 25 cents.

STROUDWATER

THE TATE HOUSE, (Page 169), Westbrook St. Built in 1755 by George Tate. Owned and operated by the National Society of Colonial Dames of American Resident in Maine. OPEN: Wednesdays 10:30 to 5, July, August and the first half of September. Closed Sundays. ADMISSION: 25 cents.

THOMASTON

MONTPELIER, (Page 208), High St., (off Route 1). A replica, built in 1929, of the original Montpelier, or Knox Mansion, (built 1795). Owned and operated by the Knox Memorial Association, Inc. OPEN: week days and Sundays 10 to 6, June through October. EXHIBITS: furniture and personal effects of Major General Henry Knox. ADMISSION: 50 cents, children accompanied by teachers admitted free.

WATERVILLE

REDINGTON MUSEUM. Built 1814 by William Redington. Owned and operated by the Waterville Historical Society. OPEN: week days, except Monday, 2 to 8, May 1 to October 31. Closed Sundays. EXHIBITS: old fashion kitchen, Indian relics, records, etc. No admission fee.

YORK VILLAGE   THE OLD GAOL, (Page 77), Main St., opposite Postoffice. Built 1653 by Massachusetts Bay Colony. Owned by the Town of York. Operated by the Old Gaol Museum Committee. OPEN: week days 9:30 to 5:30, Sundays 1 to 5:30, July 4 to September 15. EXHIBITS: old furniture, silver, pewter, costumes, letters, documents, etc. Old dungeons. ADMISSION: 30 cents, children 12 cents.

YORK VILLAGE   JEFFERDS' TAVERN, (Page 177), York Street. Built 1750 by Dominicus Lord. Moved from Wells to York in 1939. Owned and operated by the Society for the Preservation of Historic Landmarks in York County. OPEN: week days 1 to 6. Tea from 4 to 6. End of May through Labor Day. Closed Sundays. EXHIBITS: Furnishings of the period. No admission fee.

MASSACHUSETTS

ADAMS   SUSAN B. ANTHONY BIRTHPLACE, East Road at the "Four Corners," on the outskirts of Adams. Built about 1815 by Daniel Anthony. Owned and operated by the Adams Society of Friends Descendants. OPEN: the year round. Birth room furnished in keeping with a Quaker home. Custodian in charge. No admission fee.

ADAMS   ELEAZER BROWN HOMESTEAD, (Page 193), located on the outskirts of Adams on Orchard St. (Route 116). Built 1778 by Eleazer Brown. Owned and operated by the Eleazer Brown Homestead Association. OPEN: all summer, preferably in the afternoon. The house commands a fine view of the Hoosic valley. EXHIBITS: large collection of early domestic ware, books and furniture. No admission fee.

AMESBURY   MACY-COLBY HOUSE, (Page 70), Main St. Built about 1650 by Thomas Macy. Owned by the Bartlett Cemetery Association. Operated by the Josiah Bartlett Chapter, Daughters of the American Revolution. OPEN: Wednesdays 2 to 4, June through September. Furnished as a typical pioneer home. Voluntary contributions.

AMESBURY   WHITTIER HOME, (Page 242), 86 Friend St. Built before 1836, by Thomas Allen. Remodeled 1847 and 1884. Owned and operated by the Whittier Home Association. OPEN: week days 10 to 5, the year round. Closed Sundays and holidays. EXHIBITS: portraits, manuscripts, books, furniture, etc. Voluntary contributions.

AMHERST   NEHEMIAH STRONG HOUSE, 67 Amity St. Built 1744 by Nehemiah Strong. Owned and operated by the Amherst Historical Society. OPEN: Tuesday and Friday 2 to 5, May 15 to October 15, and by appointment. EXHIBITS: collections of local interest. ADMISSION: 25 cents, children 10 cents.

ANDOVER   DEACON AMOS BLANCHARD HOUSE, (Page 240), 97 Main St. Built 1819 by Deacon Amos Blanchard. Owned and operated by the Andover Historical Society. OPEN: Tuesday and Saturday 2 to 5, the year round, and by appointment. Contains hand worked mantels and staircases, and typical Andover furniture of that period. No admission fee.

ARLINGTON   JASON RUSSELL HOUSE, (Page 99), 7 Jason St. Built about 1680 by Martha Russell. Owned and operated by the Arlington Historical Society. OPEN: week days except Monday 2 to 5, April to November. Closed Sunday and Monday. EXHIBITS: bullet holes made by the British April 19, 1775, silverware executed by Paul Revere and historic souvenirs. Voluntary contributions.

ASSINIPPI JACOBS FARMHOUSE, corner Main St. and Jacobs Lane. Built in 1726 by Joshua Jacobs and brother, Dr. Joseph Jacobs. East wing added in 1839. Owned and operated by the Society for the Preservation of New England Antiquities. Mr. and Mrs. Robert Goode, custodians. OPEN: Mondays and Thursdays, 2 to 5, June 1 to October 1. EXHIBITS: fine collection of fire apparatus, dating from 1760 to the early 1900's, located in the barns. No admission fee.

BARNSTABLE CROCKER TAVERN, (Page 170), Main St. Built 1754. Owned and operated by the Society for the Preservation of New England Antiquities. Mrs. A. W. Tonks, custodian. OPEN: on application at all reasonable hours. EXHIBITS: several old rooms, furniture. ADMISSION: 25 cents.

BERNARDSTON RYTHER HOUSE, (Page 161). Built 1745 by the Ryther family. Owned and operated by F. A. and Grace M. Donaldson. OPEN: by appointment. EXHIBITS: furniture, glass, Indian relics, guns, tools, pewter, swords, prints, etc., and a wall painting, supposedly the work of a British spy. No admission fee.

BEVERLY JOHN BALCH HOUSE, (Pages 60-62), 448 Cabot St. (Route 1A). Built about 1638 by John Balch. Several subsequent additions. Owned and operated by the Beverly Historical Society. OPEN: week days, by appointment. EXHIBITS: Colonial furnishings.

BEVERLY CABOT HOUSE, (Page 193), 117 Cabot St. Built 1781 by John Cabot. Owned and operated by the Beverly Historical Society. OPEN: week days 10 to 4, during July and August; Saturdays 10 to 4 the year round. Closed Sundays. EXHIBITS: documents, portraits, glass, china, furniture, ship's logs, etc. No admission fee.

BEVERLY THE HALE HOUSE, (Page 118), 39 Hale St. Built in 1697 by Reverend John Hale. Owned and operated by the Beverly Historical Society. OPEN: week days, except Monday, 10 to 12, 2 to 5, June 15 to September 15. EXHIBITS: Nathan Hale's fire brigade bucket, antiques. Voluntary contributions.

BOSTON HARRISON GRAY OTIS HOUSE, (Pages 206, 207), 141 Cambridge St. Built 1795 by Harrison Gray Otis. Architect probably was Charles Bulfinch. Owned and operated by the Society for the Preservation of New England Antiquities. OPEN: week days 9 to 5, Saturdays 9 to 1, the year round. Closed Sundays and holidays. Appropriately furnished throughout. EXHIBITS: New England Museum with collections of costumes, glass, ceramics, silver, pewter, ship models, Shaker objects, painted ware, etc. ADMISSION: 25 cents, children under 12 free.

BOSTON PAUL REVERE HOUSE, (Page 71), 19 North Square. Built about 1650. Restored 1908. Owned and operated by the Paul Revere Memorial Association. OPEN: week days 10 to 4, the year round. Closed Sundays and holidays. ADMISSION: 30 cents, special prices for classes of school children.

BOSTON
(Dorchester) JAMES BLAKE HOUSE, (Page 70), Edward Everett Square. Built 1648. Owned and operated by the Dorchester Historical Society. OPEN: by appointment.

BOSTON
(Roxbury) DILLAWAY HOUSE, (Page 165), 183 Roxbury St. Built 1750. Owned by the City of Boston. Operated by the Roxbury Historical Society. OPEN: week days 10 to 2, the year round. Sundays 2 to 4. Once served as a parsonage for First Church. No admission fee.

BOURNE "APTUCXET", Plymouth Colony's First Trading Post, (Page 56). Shore Road, about 100 yards off the highway, well marked with signs. A replica of an early trading post, built 1930. Original built 1627. Owned and operated by the Bourne Historical Society. OPEN: daily, except Monday, 9 to 5, April 1 to November 1. EXHIBITS: relics of Pilgrim days. ADMISSION: 25 cents, children 10 cents.

BOXFORD   HOLYOKE-FRENCH HOUSE, (Page 177), corner of Elm St. and Topsfield Road. Built 1760 by Samuel Holyoke for his son the Reverend Elizur Holyoke. Restored in 1940. Owned and operated by the Boxford Historical Society. OPEN: Sunday afternoons 3 to 5, during the summer months. Week days upon special request. EXHIBITS: old chair which belonged to the Reverend Elizur Holyoke and primitive portraits. ADMISSION: 25 cents.

BROOKLINE   EDWARD DEVOTION HOUSE, (Page 161), 347 Harvard St. Built about 1740 by Edward Devotion, Sr. Owned by the Town of Brookline. Operated by the Brookline Historical Society. OPEN: Saturdays 11 to 4, the year round, and by appointment. EXHIBITS: original furniture and books, hardware and woodwork. Voluntary contributions.

CAMBRIDGE   BRATTLE HOUSE, (Page 159), 42 Brattle St. Built about 1735. Owned and operated by the Cambridge Social Union. OPEN: Monday through Friday, 9 to 5, (except when rooms are being used for courses of the Center). EXHIBITS: panelling and stairway. No admission fee.

CAMBRIDGE   COOPER-FROST-AUSTIN HOUSE, (Page 78), 21 Linnaean St. Built about 1657 by John Cooper. Owned and operated by the Society for the Preservation of New England Antiquities. OPEN: Thursdays only, 2 to 5, the year round. The oldest house in Cambridge. ADMISSION: 25 cents.

CAMBRIDGE   JOHN HICKS HOUSE, (Page 181), Boylston and South Sts. Built about 1762 by John Hicks. Owned by Harvard University. Open to visitors upon application at Kirkland House, Harvard University. This house was used as an Army office by Generals Washington and Putnam. No admission fee.

CAMBRIDGE   THE LONGFELLOW HOUSE, (Page 172), 105 Brattle St. Built 1759 by Major John Vassal. Owned by The Longfellow House Trust. Operated by Henry Wadsworth Longfellow Dana. OPEN: daily, except Monday, 3 to 5, June through October; Wednesdays, Saturdays and Sundays, 2 to 4, November through May. General Washington's Headquarters from July 1775 to April 1776. Occupied by the poet Longfellow from 1837 until his death in 1882. Here he wrote the majority of his poems. EXHIBITS: furniture, pictures, books, manuscripts, etc. ADMISSION: 30 cents, children under 12, 9 cents.

CAMBRIDGE   WADSWORTH HOUSE, (Page 152), 1341 Massachusetts Ave., opposite Holyoke St., in the Harvard Yard. Built 1726. Owned by Harvard University. OPEN: week days 9 to 5, the year round (except June through September, when it is closed Saturdays). Closed Sundays. The home of Harvard Presidents for 123 years. No admission fee.

CHATHAM   ATWOOD HOUSE, (Page 167), Stage Harbor Road. Built 1752 by Joseph Atwood. Owned and operated by the Chatham Historical Society, Inc. OPEN: Wednesday and Friday, 2 to 5, during July and August, and by appointment. Closed Sundays. EXHIBITS: old furniture and relics. Voluntary contributions.

CHELSEA   GOVERNOR BELLINGHAM-CARY HOUSE, 34 Parker St. Built 1659 by Governor Bellingham. Remodeled 1791. Owned and operated by the Cary House Association. OPEN: by appointment. EXHIBITS: Colonial stairway, secret passage, panelling, hardware, etc. Voluntary contributions.

CHESHIRE   THE COLE HOUSE, North Main St., (Route 8). Built in 1804 by Calvin Hall and John Leland, Jr. Owned and operated by Mrs. Anna F. Bennett. OPEN: week days and Sundays, 10 to 6, the year round. EXHIBITS: mural paintings of Masonic emblems on walls of second-story rooms, once used as a lodge room from 1804 to 1816. Voluntary contributions.

COHASSET

THE WILSON HOUSE, Elm St. Built in 1800 by John Wilson. Owned by William H. McGaw and operated by the Cohasset Historical Society. OPEN: Wednesday, Friday and Saturday, 12 to 5, June through August. EXHIBITS: historic items and relics.· No admission fee.

CONCORD

THE CONCORD ANTIQUARIAN SOCIETY, (Pages 245, 246), Lexington Road and Cambridge Turnpike. Built 1929 to house many fine period rooms and exhibits. Owned and operated by the Concord Antiquarian Society. OPEN: week days 10 to 5:30, Sundays 2 to 5:30, April 19 to November 11. Closed Mondays and holidays. EXHIBITS: contents of Emerson's study, a Thoreau collection, relics and diorama of the Concord fight, one of Paul Revere's lanterns, fifteen period rooms, etc. ADMISSION: 30 cents, children 18 cents.

CONCORD

EMERSON HOUSE, (Page 241), Cambridge Turnpike, opposite the Antiquarian House. Built 1829. Owned and operated by the Emerson Memorial Association. OPEN: week days 9:30 to 11:30, 1:30 to 3:30, the year round. Closed Sundays. Residence of Ralph Waldo Emerson from 1835 until his death in 1882. ADMISSION: 25 cents, children under fifteen, 15 cents.

CONCORD

THE OLD MANSE, (Page 188), on Monument St., "by the North Bridge." Built 1769 by the Reverend William Emerson, grandfather of Ralph Waldo Emerson. Owned and operated by the Trustees of Public Reservations. OPEN: week days, except Mondays, 11 to 5:30, Sundays 2 to 6, June to November. Nathaniel Hawthorne lived here from 1842 to 1845. EXHIBITS: books, furnishings, inscriptions, wall papers practically unchanged since Hawthorne's occupancy. ADMISSION: 25 cents, children 15 cents.

CONCORD

ORCHARD HOUSE, (Page 217), Lexington Road, corner Alcott Road. The home of "Little Women," composed of two old houses dating from 1650 and 1730, assembled and modernized by the Alcotts. Owned and operated by the Louisa May Alcott Memorial Association. OPEN: week days 10 to 5, Sundays 2 to 6, from April 19 to November 11. EXHIBITS: furnishings and momentos of the Alcotts. ADMISSION: 25 cents, children 15 cents.

CONCORD

THE WAYSIDE, (Page 144), Lexington Road. Built before 1717. Remodeled 1846, 1860. The home of four authors: Nathaniel Hawthorne, Bronson Alcott, Louisa May Alcott and "Margaret Sidney," author of "The Five Little Peppers." Owned and operated by Miss Margaret M. Lathrop. OPEN: week days and Sundays all day, from June 15 to September 15. Many interesting exhibits. ADMISSION: 30 cents, children between eight and twelve, 18 cents.

CONCORD

WRIGHT TAVERN, (Page 164), 2 Lexington Road. Built as a tavern in 1747. Owned by the First Parish Church. Operated by F. H. Trumbull. OPEN: daily except Monday, 10 to 8, Sundays 12 to 8, the year round. EXHIBITS: the old bar and relics of the Revolution. This tavern was the Headquarters of the British during the battle of April 19, 1775. No admission fee. Now an inn.

CUMMINGTON

WILLIAM CULLEN BRYANT HOMESTEAD, Bryant Road, just off Route 116. Built before 1794. Owned and operated by the Trustees of Public Reservations. OPEN: Monday, Wednesday and Friday, 2:30 to 5, from June 15 to September 15. EXHIBITS: old household furniture. ADMISSION: 28 cents.

DANVERS

REBECCA NURSE HOUSE, (Pages 94, 95), 149 Pine St., near the Tapleyville railroad station. Built 1678 by Francis Nurse. Owned and operated by the Society for the Preservation of New England Antiquities. Mr. and Mrs. George Gordon, custodians. OPEN: week days 10 to 5, during the summer months. Other times by appointment. EXHIBITS: several 17th Century rooms. ADMISSION: 25 cents.

DANVERS   JEREMIAH PAGE HOUSE, (Page 168), 11 Page St. Built 1754 by Captain Jeremiah Page. Owned and operated by the Danvers Historical Society. OPEN: Wednesday afternoons, and by appointment, the year round. EXHIBITS: furniture and objects of historic interest. Voluntary contributions.

DANVERS   JAMES PUTNAM HOUSE, (Page 96), 42 Summer Street. Built 1680 by James Putnam. Remodeled 1715. Owned by Mrs. Phoebe Woodman Grantham. OPEN: week days and Sundays 11 to 8, the year round. No admission fee. Now an inn.

DANVERSPORT   SAMUEL FOWLER HOUSE, (Pages 234, 235), 166 High St. Built 1810 by Samuel Fowler. Owned and operated by the Society for the Preservation of New England Antiquities. Mrs. Henry F. Twardzik, custodian. OPEN: Wednesdays 3 to 5, Saturdays 10 to 5, other times by appointment, the year round. Closed Sundays and holidays. EXHIBITS: furniture, woodwork, wall paper, in original condition and some pewter. ADMISSION: 25 cents, children accompanied by adult, free; school classes with teacher free, by appointment.

DEDHAM   FAIRBANKS HOUSE, (Pages 57, 58), 511 East St., corner Eastern Ave. Built 1636 by "Jonathan Fayerbanke" and still in original form. Owned and operated by the Fairbanks Family in America, Inc. OPEN: week days and Sundays, from 9 to 6, May 1 to November 1. EXHIBITS: family heirlooms and furniture. Voluntary contributions.

DUXBURY   JOHN ALDEN HOUSE, (Page 76), Alden St. near the railway station. Built 1653 by Jonathan Alden, third son of John and Priscilla Alden. Owned by the Alden Kindred in America. Operated by Mrs. Charles L. Alden. OPEN: week days and Sundays, 9:30 to 5:30, the year round. Hostess in attendance May 15 to October 15. EXHIBITS: furnished with Colonial antiques. ADMISSION: 25 cents, children under ten, free.

DUXBURY   ALEXANDER STANDISH HOUSE, Standish St. Built in 1666 by Alexander Standish and remodeled in 1946. Owned by David L. Patten. Visitors can see house when owner is in residence. EXHIBITS: old panelling, kitchen beams, pewter, etc.

EDGARTOWN   ESQUIRE THOMAS COOKE HOUSE, (Page 184), corner Cooke and School Sts. Built 1766 by Thomas Cooke. Reconditioned 1931. Owned and operated by the Dukes County Historical Society. OPEN: Wednesday, Saturday and Sunday, 2 to 5, in summer. Wednesday and Saturday, 2 to 5, remainder of the year. EXHIBITS: collections of Vineyard literature, art and natural history. No admission fee.

FAIRHAVEN   CAPTAIN THOMAS BENNETT HOUSE, 199 Main St. Built 1810 by Captain Thomas Bennett. Owned and operated by the Society for the Preservation of New England Antiquities. OPEN: week days 9 to 5, the year round. Sundays by appointment. Mrs. Charlotte B. Spooner, custodian. ADMISSION: 25 cents.

FALMOUTH   JULIA A. WOOD HOUSE, (Page 203), Palmer Ave. opposite the Village Green. Built about 1790. Owned and operated by the Falmouth Historical Society. OPEN: Tuesday through Friday, 1 to 5, Saturday 10 to 2, from July 1 to September 10. Closed Sundays. EXHIBITS: glassware, costumes, furniture, relics of whaling ships, War of 1812, etc. ADMISSION: 25 cents, children 15 cents.

GLOUCESTER   JAMES BABSON COOPERAGE SHOP, (Page 79), Route 127 between Rockport and Gloucester. Built 1659 by James Babson. Owned by the City of Gloucester. Operated by the Rockport Garden Club. OPEN: Saturday 3 to 5, during July and August. Furnished as in 1700, with original copper, cooperage and other tools. No admission fee.

GLOUCESTER   "BEAUPORT," Eastern Point Road. Built in 1907 by Henry Torry. Owned and operated by the Society for the Preservation of New England Antiquities. Mr. and Mrs. Joseph McMullen, custodians. OPEN: week days, except holidays, 2:30 to 5:30, June 1 to October 1. EXHIBITS: fifty-six completely furnished rooms, including a New England pine kitchen, round circular library and a Jacobean room. ADMISSION: $1.00, children 50 cents.

GLOUCESTER   CAPE ANN HISTORICAL HOUSE, (Page 231), 27 Pleasant St. Built about 1805. Owned and operated by the Cape Ann Scientific, Literary and Historical Association. OPEN: week days 11 to 4, June 15 to September 15. EXHIBITS: ship models and documents, large collection of shells and minerals, old furniture, etc. ADMISSION: 25 cents.

GLOUCESTER   SARGENT-MURRAY-GILMAN-HOUGH HOUSE, (Page 187), 49 Middle St. Built 1768 by Winthrop Sargent. Remodeled 1917. Owned and operated by the Sargent-Murray-Gilman-Hough House Association. OPEN: week days 11 to 6, July and August, closed Sundays. EXHIBITS: wood panelling, furniture and portraits. ADMISSION: 25 cents.

GREAT BARRINGTON   WILLIAM CULLEN BRYANT HOUSE, (Page 173), in the courtyard of the Berkshire Inn, 362 Main St. Built 1759 by General Joseph Dwight. Owned and operated by Olde Egremont, Inc. OPEN: week days and Sundays, May 1 to November 1. EXHIBITS: furniture, panelling, old fireplaces. No admission fee.

GROTON   THE GOVERNOR BOUTWELL HOUSE, Main St., opposite Town Hall. Built in 1851 by Governor George S. Boutwell. Remodeled 1938. Owned and operated by the Groton Historical Society. OPEN: Saturday afternoons, 3 to 5, June to October inclusive. EXHIBITS: historical relics and some pieces of fine old furniture. No admission fee.

HADLEY   OLDE HADLEY FARM MUSEUM, (Page 194), near the old Meeting House. A remodeled barn, originally built in 1782. Owned and operated by Henry and Clifton Johnson. OPEN: Saturday and Sunday 2 to 5, May to November. No admission fee.

HANOVER CENTER   "DRUMMER" SAMUEL STETSON HOUSE, (Page 116), near the Village Green, off Route 3. Built about 1694. Enlarged before 1716 by "Drummer" Samuel Stetson. Owned and operated by the Society for the Preservation of New England Antiquities. Mr. and Mrs. Ronald Conant, custodians. OPEN: week days 10 to 5, the year round. Sundays by appointment. ADMISSION: 25 cents.

HARVARD   FRUITLANDS AND THE WAYSIDE MUSEUMS, INC., (Page 146), on Prospect Hill, (follow the signs from the town square). Founded by Miss Clara Endicott Sears. OPEN: week days except Monday 12:30 to 6:30, Sundays 12:30 to 6:30, May 30 to October 1. Group includes FRUITLANDS (built before 1717), SHAKER HOUSE (1781), THE AMERICAN INDIAN MUSEUM, and tea room. ADMISSION: 10 cents to each house.

HAVERHILL   "THE BUTTONWOODS," (Page 238), 240 Water St. adjacent to John Ward House. Built 1814 by James Duncan Jr. for his son, Samuel Duncan. Owned and operated by the Haverhill Historical Society. OPEN: Tuesday, Thursday and Saturday 2 to 5, the year round. Open on Sunday by special arrangement only. EXHIBITS: books, manuscripts, period furniture, letters, scalping knives, etc. Voluntary contributions.

HAVERHILL   JOHN WARD HOUSE, (Page 66), 240 Water St. Built before 1645 by Reverend John Ward. Remodeled 1943-44. Owned and operated by the Haverhill Historical Society. OPEN: Tuesday, Thursday and Saturday 2 to 5, the year round. Open on Sunday by special arrangement only. Furnished as a 17th Century home. Voluntary contributions.

HAVERHILL JOHN GREENLEAF WHITTIER HOMESTEAD, (Page 109), Whittier Road, East Haverhill, on Route 110 between Haverhill and Merrimac, (marked with signs). Built 1688 by Thomas Whittier. Birthplace of the New England poet. OPEN: week days except Monday, 10 to 5:30, Sundays 12:30 to 5, the year round. ADMISSION: 10 cents.

HINGHAM OLD ORDINARY, (Page 74), Lincoln St. Built 1650. Owned and operated by the Hingham Historical Society. OPEN: week days 2 to 5, April 19 to November 1. A fine example of an early wayside inn. ADMISSION: 25 cents.

IPSWICH EMERSON-HOWARD HOUSE, (Pages 68, 69), 41 Turkey Shore Road at eastern end of Green St. bridge. Said to have been built before 1648 by Thomas Emerson. Owned and operated by the Society for the Preservation of New England Antiquities. Mrs. Sarah Goodale, custodian. OPEN: at reasonable hours the year round. EXHIBITS: period furnishings. ADMISSION: 25 cents.

IPSWICH 1640 HART HOUSE, (Page 65), corner Linebrook Road and Kimball Ave. Restored 1902 by Ralph W. Burnham. Owned and operated by Arthur F. Edes. OPEN: 9 a.m. to 9 p.m. during the warm months. EXHIBITS: old furniture and interiors. The parlor was chosen by the Metropolitan Museum as one of the finest examples of early 17th Century architecture in America. ADMISSION: 25 cents. If dining room or gift shop is patronized, admission is free.

IPSWICH THE ROGER PRESTON-REGINALD FOSTER HOUSE, 6 Water St. Built about 1640. Owned and operated by the Society for the Preservation of New England Antiquities. Mr. and Mrs. Howard Von Suck, custodians. OPEN: at all reasonable hours. EXHIBITS: mainly of architectural interest. ADMISSION: 25 cents.

IPSWICH THE WHIPPLE HOUSE, (Pages 64, 65), 53 South Main St. Original part built 1638-40 by John Fawn. Additions in 1670 built by Captain John Whipple and lean-to about 1700 by Major John Whipple. Owned and operated by the Ipswich Historical Society. OPEN: week days except Monday, 10 to 6, Sundays 1 to 6, the year round. EXHIBITS: 17th Century and 18th Century furniture, books, china, early interiors, genealogical records, etc. Voluntary contributions.

KINGSTON MAJOR JOHN BRADFORD HOUSE, (Pages 90, 91), Landing Road, near Routes 3 and 3A. Built 1674 by Major William Bradford. Remodeled 1720. Restored 1921. Owned and operated by the Jones River Village Club, Inc. OPEN: week days 9:30 to 5:30, from July 1 through Labor Day. Sundays by appointment only. Furnished in the manner of an authentic Pilgrim home. ADMISSION: 25 cents, children 10 cents.

KINGSTON OLD BREWSTER HOUSE, (Page 113), Brewster Road, (marked by a sign about 150 yards south of the intersection of Routes 3 and 3A). Built 1690 by William Bradford, son of Governor Bradford. Owned and operated by Edward L. Singsen. OPEN: week days 10 to 5, June to October. EXHIBITS: period furniture, doll's house, relics of the Brewster family since the Mayflower, etc. ADMISSION: 30 cents, children 15 cents.

LEXINGTON BUCKMAN TAVERN, (Pages 114, 115), facing the Battle Green. Built about 1690. Owned by the Town of Lexington. Operated by the Lexington Historical Society. OPEN: week days 10 to 5, Sundays 2 to 4, April 19 to November 11. This was the rendezvous of the Minute-Men April 19, 1775. EXHIBITS: old bar, furnishings and relics of historic interest. Voluntary contributions.

LEXINGTON | HANCOCK-CLARKE HOUSE, (Pages 118, 119), 35 Hancock St. Built 1698 by Reverend John Hancock. Enlarged 1734. Owned and operated by the Lexington Historical Society. OPEN: week days 9:30 to 5, Sundays 2 to 4, April 1 to November 1. (During March: week days 11 to 4, Sundays 2 to 4). John Hancock and Sam Adams were sleeping here when aroused by Paul Revere, April 19, 1775. EXHIBITS: extensive collection of Revolutionary relics. Voluntary contributions.

LEXINGTON | MUNROE TAVERN, (Page 117), 1332 Massachusetts Ave. Built 1695 by William Munroe. Owned and operated by the Lexington Historical Society. OPEN: week days 9:30 to 5, Sundays 2 to 5, April 19 to November 11. This tavern was Earl Percy's Headquarters and Hospital, April 19, 1775. EXHIBITS: collection of Revolutionary relics. Voluntary contributions.

LINCOLN | HARTWELL FARM, (Page 59), Virginia Road, just off the main highway between Lexington and Concord. Built 1636-39 by William Hartwell. Owned and operated by Marion Fitch and Jane Poor. OPEN: week days except Monday, 12 to 7:30, Sundays 12 to 5:30, the year round. No admission fee. Now an inn.

LONGMEADOW | RICHARD SALTER STORRS PARSONAGE, (Page 200), 697 Longmeadow St. Built 1786 by Richard Salter Storrs. Owned by the Richard Storrs Library Association and operated by the Longmeadow Historical Society. OPEN: Thursday 2 to 5, August and September. EXHIBITS: antiques. No admission fee.

LOWELL | WHISTLER HOUSE, 243 Worthen St. Built 1823-24 by Captain John Bassett. Owned and operated by the Lowell Art Association. OPEN: week days except Monday, 10 to 5, Sundays 1:30 to 5, the year round, except August. The birthplace of James McNeill Whistler. EXHIBITS: Whistler souvenirs and works by his contemporary artists. No admission fee.

LYNN | HYDE-MILLS HOUSE, 125 Green St. Built about 1838 by Daniel Hyde and William N. Mills. Owned and operated by the Lynn Historical Society. OPEN: one afternoon a week 2 to 5, during July and August, and by appointment. EXHIBITS: furniture, china, glass, silver, pewter and an early Lynn shoe shop. No admission fee.

MANCHESTER | TRASK HOUSE, (Page 241), 12 Union St., opposite the Public Library. Built about 1830 by Captain Richard Trask, Restored 1933. Owned and operated by the Manchester Historical Society. OPEN: Wednesdays 3 to 5, during July and August, and by appointment. No admission fee.

MANSFIELD | FISHER-RICHARDSON HOUSE, (Page 142), Willow St. on the southern outskirts of the town. Built 1704 by Ebenezer Hall. Additions made 1800. Restored 1930. Owned and operated by the Town of Mansfield. OPEN: Saturday and Sunday 2 to 5, June 15 to October 1. Furnishings of the period. No admission fee.

MARBLEHEAD | KING HOOPER MANSION, (Pages 162, 163), 8 Hooper St. Built 1745 by Robert Hooper. Rear wing dates from an earlier epoch. Owned and operated by the Marblehead Arts Association. OPEN: week days, except Monday, 2 to 5, the year round. Sundays 2 to 5. EXHIBITS: period furniture, old panelling and stairs, banquet hall, (now gallery). A fine example of the type of house built by merchant princes of the 18th Century. ADMISSION: 30 cents.

MARBLEHEAD | LEE MANSION, (Pages 185, 186), 161 Washington St. Built 1768 by Colonel Jeremiah Lee. Owned and operated by the Marblehead Historical Society. OPEN: week days 9 to 5, April to December. Sundays 3 to 5, July through October. EXHIBITS: furniture, china, glass, hand painted wall paper, carved stair rail, etc. ADMISSION: 30 cents, children 15 cents, under twelve, free.

MARSHFIELD WINSLOW HOUSE, (Page 120), corner Careswell and Webster Sts. Built 1699 by Honorable Isaac Winslow. Remodeled about 1756. Owned and operated by the Historic Winslow House Association. OPEN: week days and Sundays, 10 to 6. June 15 to September 15. EXHIBITS: children's room, Daniel Webster room. ADMISSION: 30 cents, children 15 cents.

MEDFORD ROYALL HOUSE, (Pages 155, 156), 15 George St. Earliest part built 1638 by Governor John Winthrop. Enlarged by Lt. Governor John Usher about 1700. Further enlarged by Colonel Isaac Royall 1732. Owned and operated by the Royall House Association. OPEN: Tuesday, Wednesday, Thursday and Saturday 2 to 5, Sundays 2 to 5, from May 1 to October 1. Furnishings of the period. ADMISSION: 25 cents, children 15 cents.

MEDFORD PETER TUFTS HOUSE, (Page 96), 350 Riverside Ave. near Spring St. Built about 1678 by Captain Peter Tufts. Owned and operated by the Society for the Preservation of New England Antiquities. Mr. and Mrs. Alfred Bicknell, custodians. OPEN: at reasonable hours. Closed Sundays. ADMISSION: 25 cents.

MELROSE PHINEAS UPHAM HOUSE, (Page 141), 253 Upham St. Built 1703 by Phineas Upham. Restored 1914. Owned and operated by the Melrose Historical Society. OPEN: by appointment. (apply next door or at 643 Main St.) EXHIBITS: interiors of the period. No admission fee.

MILTON GOVERNOR BELCHER PLACE, 401 Adams St. Built in 1777 by the widow of Governor Jonathan Belcher. Owned by the Milton Historical Society. OPEN: by appointment.

NANTUCKET JETHRO COFFIN HOUSE, (Page 107), Sunset Road. The oldest house in Nantucket. Built 1686 by Peter Coffin. Restored 1926. Owned and operated by the Nantucket Historical Association. OPEN: week days 9:30 to 5:30, Sundays 1:30 to 5, June 20 to September 15. ADMISSION: 25 cents.

NANTUCKET MARIA MITCHELL MEMORIAL HOUSE, (Page 204), 1 Vestal St. Built 1790 by Hezekiah Swain and brother. Owned and operated by the Nantucket Maria Mitchell Association. OPEN: week days 10 to 12, 2 to 5, June 15 to September 15. Closed Sundays. EXHIBITS: wild flowers, Nantucket birds and shells, scientific library, astronomical observatory, etc. ADMISSION: 25 cents.

NEWBURY THE TRISTRAM COFFIN HOUSE, (Pages 72-74), 14 High St. Original ell built about 1651. Owned and operated by the Society for the Preservation of New England Antiquities. Mr. and Mrs. William H. MacHugh, custodians. OPEN: Monday, Wednesday and Friday, 2 to 5, the year round. EXHIBITS: interiors of the period. ADMISSION: 25 cents.

NEWBURY SHORT HOUSE, (Page 157), 33 High Road. Built 1733. Owned and operated by the Society for the Preservation of New England Antiquities. Mr. and Mrs. George Otis Mudge, custodians. OPEN: week days 10 to 5. Sundays by appointment. EXHIBITS: fine old panelling and some furniture. ADMISSION: 25 cents.

NEWBURY SWETT-ILLSLEY HOUSE, (Page 89), 4-6 High Road. Built before 1670 by Stephen Swett. Owned and operated by the Society for the Preservation of New England Antiquities. OPEN: March 19 through Christmas. Closed Saturdays and Mondays. Partly used as a tea room by Miss Lillian J. Franklin. EXHIBITS: old woodwork, fireplaces and tap room.

NEWBURYPORT BRADBURY-SPALDING HOUSE, 28 Green St. Built 1788-1791. Owned and operated by the Society for the Preservation of New England Antiquities. Mr. and Mrs. Allen Dodge, custodians. OPEN: Monday, Wednesday and Friday, 10 to 5. Other times by appointment. EXHIBITS: paintings, prints and old furniture. ADMISSION: 25 cents.

NEWBURYPORT   PETTINGELL-FOWLER HOUSE, (Page 205), 164 High St., corner Winter St. Built about 1792 by John Pettingell. Owned and operated by the Historical Society of Old Newbury. OPEN: week days 2 to 5, June 1 to October 1. Closed Sundays. EXHIBITS: ship models, combs, dolls, costumes, portraits, etc. ADMISSION: 10 cents, children free.

NEWBURYPORT   TRACY HOUSE, 94 State St. Built 1771 by Patrick Tracy for his son Nathaniel, Simpson Annex (Reading Room) added in 1880. Owned by the City of Newburyport. OPEN: daily except Sunday 9 a.m. to 9 p.m. EXHIBITS: 18th Century furniture and Gilbert Stuart portrait. No admission fee.

NORTH ANDOVER   NORTH ANDOVER HISTORICAL SOCIETY COTTAGE AND SAMUEL DALE STEVENS MEMORIAL BUILDING, (Page 204), 153 Academy Road. The Cottage was built in 1796 and the Museum in 1932. Owned and operated by the North Andover Historical Society. OPEN: Monday, Wednesday and Saturday, 2 to 5, May 1 to November 1. EXHIBITS: pewter, early textile appliances, laces, gowns and accessories, Indian relics, etc. The "Cottage" is completely furnished in the style of 100 and more years ago. No admission fee.

NORTH OXFORD   CLARA BARTON BIRTHPLACE, (Page 230), on Clara Barton Road between Route 12 and Route 20. Built about 1804 by Stephen Barton, father of Clara Barton. Owned and operated by the Association of Universalist Women. OPEN: week days and Sunday, the year round. EXHIBITS: relics concerning Clara Barton's life. ADMISSION: 25 cents, smaller children free.

NORTHAMPTON   CAPEN HOUSE, Prospect St. Built 1825 by Judge Howe and in 1883 was adapted for a dormitory for the Capen School. Owned by Smith College. OPEN: at reasonable hours during the academic year.

NORTHAMPTON   ISAAC DAMON HOUSE, (Page 238), 46 Bridge St. Built 1812 by Isaac Damon. Remodeled about 1825. Owned and operated by the Northampton Historical Society. OPEN: Wednesday, 2:30 to 5, during summer months. Other times by appointment. Apply at Parsons House, next door. EXHIBITS: Isaac Damon's architects draughting instruments, model of one of his bridges, medals for his best model of bridges, music room displaying the souvenirs of the musical life of Northampton and a collection of Jenny Lind articles. Voluntary contributions.

NORTHAMPTON   DEWEY HOUSE, on the old campus. Built 1827 by Judge Charles A. Dewey. Remodeled 1874 and 1898. Owned by Smith College. OPEN: October to June 15 or during the academic year. Now used as a dormitory. It was the first college house.

NORTHAMPTON   CORNET JOSEPH PARSON HOUSE, (Page 79), 58 Bridge St. Built 1658 by Cornet Joseph Parsons. Remodeled about 1806. Owned and operated by the Northampton Historical Society. EXHIBITS: portraits, old prints daguerreotypes, photographs, furniture, china, glass, hand-woven linens, bedspreads, quilts, embroideries, lace, costumes, documents, books, wooden-ware, tinware, fire-arms, pewter and silver. OPEN: Wednesday, Friday and Sunday, 2 to 5, the year round. Voluntary contributions.

NORTHAMPTON   SESSIONS HOUSE, Elm St. Built 1700 by Lieutenant Jonathan Hunt. Owned by Smith College. OPEN: at reasonable hours during academic year. The house has a secret staircase said to have been used by General Burgoyne.

NORTHAMPTON   WIGGINS COUNTRY STORE, (Page 245), 22 Court St. Owned by Wiggins Old Tavern, Inc., and operated by Wiggins Hotel, Inc. OPEN: all year round, 7 a.m. until midnight. EXHIBITS: antique shop, country store, loom room, court yard, etc. No admission fee.

NORWOOD — THE DAY HOUSE, 93 Day St. Built about 1860 by Lewis Day. Remodeled 1895. Owned and operated by the Norwood Historical Society. OPEN: by appointment. EXHIBITS: antique furniture, genealogical charts and data pertinent to Norwood. No admission fee.

OLD DEERFIELD — FRARY HOUSE, (Page 110), Built 1685 by Samson Frary. Owned and operated by the Pocumtuck Valley Memorial Association. OPEN: daily except Monday, 9 to 12, 1 to 5, from June 25 through Labor Day and Saturday and Sundays 1 to 5, from May to October 13. EXHIBITS: fine interiors, restored ball room. ADMISSION: 25 cents, children 10 cents.

OLD DEERFIELD — INDIAN HOUSE MEMORIAL, (Page 120), Old Deerfield St. Built 1929 as an exact reproduction of the Old Indian House built by John Sheldon in 1698. Owned by the Town of Old Deerfield. Operated by the Indian House Memorial, Inc. OPEN: week days except Monday, 9 to 5, Sundays 1 to 5, May through October. EXHIBITS: Colonial furniture, fireplaces, Indian relics, etc. ADMISSION: 10 cents, children under seven free.

OLD DEERFIELD — THE OLD MANSE, or "Willard House," (Page 188), Main St., opposite the old Brick Church. Built 1694 by Joseph Barnard. Restored 1768. Owned by the Deerfield Academy. OPEN: throughout the year upon request at the Academy office. EXHIBITS: old fireplaces, ironwork, wall paper and furniture. No admission fee. (The John Williams House (1707), Ephraim Williams House (1760) and the Nims House (about 1710) can also be visited by request at the Academy office).

OLD DEERFIELD — OLD BLOODY BROOK TAVERN, (Page 109), located behind the Indian House, Old Deerfield St. Built prior to 1700 by the Deerfield settlers (Garrison commandeered by Nathan Frary). Remodeled 1932. Owned by the Indian House Memorial, Inc., operated by Mr. and Mrs. Stephen G. Maniatty. OPEN: week days and Sundays 9 to 5, May to October inclusive. EXHIBITS: paintings and pottery. No admission fee.

PEABODY — GENERAL GIDEON FOSTER HOUSE, (Page 221), 35 Washington St. Built 1800 by General Foster. Owned and operated by the Peabody Historical Society. OPEN: Wednesdays 2 to 5, or by appointment, during the month of July. EXHIBITS: furniture, pottery, etc. No admission fee.

PLYMOUTH — ANTIQUARIAN HOUSE, (Page 233), 126 Water St. Built 1809 by Major William Hamatt. Ell aded in 1830. Owned and operated by the Plymouth Antiquarian Society. OPEN: daily except Monday, 10 to 5, July 1 through Labor Day. EXHIBITS: furniture, china, costumes, children's toys of early 19th Century. ADMISSION: 30 cents, children 18 cents.

PLYMOUTH — WILLIAM HARLOW HOUSE, (Page 92), 119 Sandwich St. (Route 3). Built 1677 by Sergeant William Harlow. Restored 1921. Owned and operated by the Plymouth Antiquarian Society. OPEN: week days and Sunday 10 to 5, July 1 through Labor Day (approximately). EXHIBITS: early furniture and household utensils. Demonstrations of 17th Century household industries: weaving, spinning, cooking, dyeing, candle making, culture and preparation of flax. ADMISSION: 30 cents, children 18 cents. Here in early May is given a Pageant of the Corn Planting.

PLYMOUTH — KENDALL HOLMES HOUSE, (Page 77), 8 Winter St. Built 1653 by William Harlow. Ell added about 1890. Owned and operated by Mr. and Mrs. Knowlton B. Holmes. EXHIBITS: antique furniture. This is the first homestead of William Harlow. OPEN: week days 11 to 4, Sundays 1 to 4, April 1 to December 1. ADMISSION: 30 cents, children 16 cents.

PLYMOUTH	THE JABEZ HOWLAND HOUSE, (Page 84), Sandwich St. (Route 3). Built 1666 by Jacob Mitchell. Restored 1941. Owned by Pilgrim John Howland Association. This is the oldest house in Plymouth. OPEN: week days and Sunday 9 to 5, June 1 to November 1. EXHIBITS: early diamond-shaped window glass, flints, bullets, pottery and other relics. ADMISSION: 30 cents, children 16 cents.
PLYMOUTH	MAYFLOWER SOCIETY HOUSE, (Page 167), corner Winslow St. and North St. Built 1754 by Edward Winslow, grandson of Governor Edward Winslow of the Mayflower. Owned and operated by the General Society of Mayflower Descendants. OPEN: daily except Monday, 10 to 5, June until into October if not too cold. EXHIBITS: Queen Anne and early Chippendale furniture.
QUINCY	JOHN ADAMS BIRTHPLACE, (Page 99), 129 Franklin St. Built about 1660. Restored 1896. Owned by the City of Quincy and operated by the Adams Chapter, Daughters of the American Revolution. OPEN: week days and Sundays 10 to 5, during the summer and from 10 until dark in winter. EXHIBITS: early Colonial furniture, old French wall paper, the old Adams cradle, personal belongings of John and Abigail Adams. ADMISSION: 30 cents, children 12 cents.
QUINCY	JOHN QUINCY ADAMS BIRTHPLACE, (Page 82), 131 Franklin St., corner President's Ave. Built 1663. Restored 1896. Owned by the City of Quincy. Operated by the Quincy Historical Society. OPEN: week days and Sunday 10 to 5, April 1 to November 1. EXHIBITS: china, early kitchen, law office used by John Adams. ADMISSION: 30 cents, children 12 cents.
QUINCY	ADAMS MANSION, (Page 154), 135 Adams St. Built 1731 by Major Leonard Vassall. Several additions during the 19th Century. Owned and operated by the Adams Memorial Society, Inc. OPEN: week days and Sundays 9 to 6, April 19 to October 30. Home of Presidents John Adams and John Quincy Adams. Occupied by the Adams family until 1927, then opened to the public as a memorial to them, with portraits and family furniture left as when occupied.
QUINCY	DOROTHY QUINCY HOMESTEAD, (Page 142), Butler Road. Built 1636, 1700 by William Coddington. Remodeled 1706 by Judge Edmund Quincy. Owned by Metropolitan Park Commission. Operated by the Massachusetts Society of Colonial Dames. OPEN: week days 10 to 6, May to November. EXHIBITS: period furniture.
READING	PARKER TAVERN, (Page 116), 99 Washington St., near the railway station. Built 1694 by Abraham Bryant. Owned and operated by the Reading Antiquarian Society. OPEN: Sundays only, 2 to 4, July and August. Furnished as an early Colonial home. No admission fee.
ROCKPORT (Pigeon Cove)	THE OLD CASTLE, (Page 145), Castle Lane. Built 1715. Lean-to added 1792. Owned and operated by the Pigeon Cove Village Improvement Society. OPEN: Saturdays and Sundays 2 to 5, during July and August. EXHIBITS: furniture and utensils of early date. No admission fee.
ROWLEY	CHAPLIN-CLARKE-WILLIAMS HOUSE, (Page 90), Bradford St. (Route 133), between Newburyport Turnpike and Old Bay Road. Built about 1671 by Joseph Chaplin. Owned and operated by the Society for the Preservation of New England Antiquities. Mrs. Katherine Marshall, custodian. OPEN: by appointment. ADMISSION: 15 cents.
ROWLEY	PLATTS-BRADSTREET HOUSE, (Page 93), Main St. Built before 1677. Restored in the 18th Century and in 1919. Owned and operated by the Rowley Historical Society. OPEN: by appointment. EXHIBITS: relics from the early days of Rowley, English garden, shoe shop, etc.

SALEM　　RETIRE BECKETT HOUSE, (Page 88), 54 Turner St. in the grounds of the House of Seven Gables. Built 1655 by John Beckett. Restored 1924. Owned and operated by the House of Seven Gables Settlement Association. OPEN: week days 10 to 6, from June to October. Closed Sundays. EXHIBITS: antiques.

SALEM　　THE STEPHEN DANIELS HOUSE, (Page 84), 1 Daniels St. at corner of Essex St. Built 1667 by Stephen Daniels. Wing added in 1756. Restored 1946. Owned and operated as an inn by Mr. and Mrs. T. P. Haller. OPEN: week days, except Friday, and Sunday, at all reasonable hours. EXHIBITS: old fireplaces, fine antique furniture. No admission fee.

SALEM　　DERBY HOUSE, (Pages 179, 180), 168 Derby St. Built 1762 by Richard Derby for his son's occupancy. Owned by the Federal Government. Operated by the National Park Service, Department of the Interior. OPEN: week days 10 to 5, the year round. Sundays 12 to 5. Closed on National holidays. The oldest brick house in Salem. EXHIBITS: old furniture, staircase, and painted panelling. ADMISSION: 30 cents, children under 17, free. Free admission to students under 19, if in school groups.

SALEM　　EAST INDIA HOUSE, (Page 192), 384 Essex St. Formerly Dean-Sprague-Stearns House. Built 1706 by Joseph Dean. Remodeled 1774-1780. Owned and operated by F. B. Ballou. OPEN: daily, the year round, (first floor only). EXHIBITS: Tory hide-out in chimney, powder and wig rooms, early McIntire panelling. Now an inn.

SALEM　　HOUSE OF SEVEN GABLES, (Pages 85, 86), 54 Turner St. Built 1668 by Captain John Turner. Restored 1910. Owned and operated by the House of Seven Gables Settlement Association. Proceeds from this house, the Hathaway House and the Retire Beckett House go to settlement work. OPEN: week days and Sundays 10 to 5 during the winter, 10 to 6 in the summer, except Thanksgiving Day and Christmas. EXHIBITS: furniture, china, kitchen utensils, secret staircase, etc. ADMISSION: 25 cents.

SALEM　　HATHAWAY HOUSE, (Page 87), 54 Turner St., in the grounds of the House of Seven Gables. Built 1682 by Benjamin Hooper. Restored 1911. Owned and operated by the House of Seven Gables Settlement Association. OPEN: week days and Sundays, 10 to 5, July and August. EXHIBITS: two rooms furnished as in the 17th Century. ADMISSION: to these rooms, 10 cents.

SALEM　　LYE SHOE SHOP, (Page 244), in the grounds of the Essex Institute, 132 Essex St. Owned and operated by the Essex Institute. OPEN: week days 9 to 5, May 1 to November 1. Closed Sundays. EXHIBITS: shoe maker's equipment of about 1830. No admission fee.

SALEM　　PEIRCE-NICHOLS HOUSE, (Page 195), 80 Federal St. Built 1782. Designed by Samuel McIntire. Owned and operated by the Essex Institute. OPEN: Wednesdays and Saturdays 2 to 5, the year round. The finest example of McIntire's wood carving. Furnishings of the period. ADMISSION: 50 cents, children (must be accompanied by an adult), 15 cents.

SALEM　　PINGREE HOUSE, (Pages 226-229), 128 Essex St. Built 1804. Designed by Samuel McIntire. Owned and operated by the Essex Institute. OPEN: week days 9 to 4:30, the year round. Closed Sundays. A Salem merchant's home, completely furnished with period pieces. EXHIBITS: fine examples of McIntire wood carving, and superb furnishings. ADMISSION: 60 cents, children (must be accompanied by an adult), 30 cents.

SALEM   THE PIONEER'S VILLAGE, (Pages 55, 56), Forest River Park, one block east of Route 1A. A reproduction of the wilderness settlement of Salem in 1630. Built by the Salem Park Department. Owned and operated by the City of Salem. OPEN: daily until dusk, June 15 to November 11. EXHIBITS: primitive habitations, a full size model of the "Arbella." The Ruck House, oldest house on record in Salem has been reconstructed as part of the group. AD MISSION: 25 cents, children 15 cents.

SALEM   ROPES MANSION, (Pages 148, 149), 318 Essex St. Built 1719. Additions built 1807 and 1894. Administered by the Trustees of the Ropes Memorial. OPEN: week days except Monday, 2 to 5, May 1 to December. Closed Sundays. EXHIBITS: double set "Canton" china, imported table glass, furniture, portraits, documents, silver, laces, etc. ADMISSION: 25 cents, children 10 cents.

SALEM   JOHN WARD HOUSE, (Page 103), in the grounds of the Essex Institute, 132 Essex St. Built 1684. Moved to this location and restored 1911. Owned and operated by the Essex Institute. OPEN: week days 9 to 4:30, May 1 to November 1. Closed Sundays. EXHIBITS: 17th Century furniture, early 19th Century shop, apothecary shop of about 1830, etc. ADMISSION: 30 cents, children 15 cents.

SALEM   THE WITCH HOUSE, (Page 80), corner of Essex and North Sts. Built before 1662. Remodeled 1674-75. Restored 1947-48. Owned and operated by Historic Salem, Inc. OPEN: daily during the summer months. EXHIBITS: authentic interiors and period furnishings.

SAUGUS   OLD IRONWORKS HOUSE, (Page 67), 235-237 Central St. Built before 1640 by Thomas Dexter. Restored 1915. Owned by the Town of Saugus. Operated by the First Iron Work Association, Inc. OPEN: at all reasonable hours. EXHIBITS: remarkable 17th Century rooms, with fine furnishings of the same period. Voluntary contributions.

SAUGUS   "SCOTCH"-BOARDMAN HOUSE, (Pages 75, 76), Howard St. Turn East at Main St. Saugus on Route 1 and cross Lynn Fells Parkway. This house is just beyond. Built 1651. OPEN: by appointment. EXHIBITS: early staircase, sponge painting, and much original sheathing. ADMISSION: 15 cents.

SCITUATE   CUDWORTH HOUSE, (Page 151), First Parish Road, Scituate Center, opposite the schoolhouse. Built 1723 by Zephaniah Cudworth. Owned by the Town of Scituate. Operated by the Scituate Historical Society. OPEN: week days 10:30 to 5, July 1 through Labor Day. Closed Sundays. Voluntary contributions.

SOUTH EGREMONT   OLD EGREMONT TAVERN, (Page 154), on Routes 23 and 41, in the center of South Egremont. Built 1730. Restored 1928. Owned and operated by Rudolph W. Schrader. OPEN: the year round as an inn. Always open to the public.

SOUTH LEE   MERRELL'S TAVERN, (Page 178), Main St. Built about 1760. Owned and operated by the Society for the Preservation of New England Antiquities. OPEN: by appointment, May to November. Contains tap room with old bar and much of the original furniture.

SOUTH SUDBURY   THE GOULDING HOUSE, (Page 141), Concord Road. Built between 1700 and 1725. Owned and operated by Leonard P. Goulding. OPEN: the year round. EXHIBITS: early New England furniture. The house has been very carefully restored with casement windows and has early panelling and woodwork, a large early stone fireplace and a fine collection of early ironwork. No admission fee.

SOUTH SUDBURY LONGFELLOW'S WAYSIDE INN, (Pages 104-107), Post Road, (Route 20), marked with signs. Built 1686 by Samuel Howe. Owned and operated by the Wayside Inn. OPEN: week days and Sundays 8 a.m. to 8 p.m. the year round. Furnished as an old time inn, and still operating as such. Other buildings of interest: Coach House, The Red Stone School House, The Grist Mill, etc. ADMISSION: 30 cents, Students 5 cents (tax only), children under twelve free.

SOUTH WORTHINGTON "EAGLE'S NEST," Birthplace of Reverend Russell H. Conwell, Conwell Road. Built around 1790 by Mr. Annabel. Owned by Leon M. Conwell and operated by Nima Conwell Tuttle. OPEN: daily, from July through September. EXHIBITS: large barn containing the exact replicas of the drawing-room and dining room of his residence on Broad St. ADMISSION: 25 cents.

STOCKBRIDGE MISSION HOUSE, (Page 158), Main St. Built 1739 for John Sergeant, first missionary to the Stockbridge Indians. Restored by Miss Mabel Choate. Owned by the Stockbridge Mission House Association. Operated by the Board of Trustees. OPEN: week days 10 to 12:30, 2 to 6, Sundays 2:30 to 6, during summer months. In winter months visitors admitted by ringing bell at Cobbler's shop. Closing hour earlier in winter. Mission House is completely furnished in the period of early America. EXHIBITS: Indian Room, Weaving Room, Courtyard, Old Fashioned Garden, etc. ADMISSION: 25 cents, children 15 cents.

STORROWTOWN (West Springfield) NEW ENGLAND COLONIAL VILLAGE, (Pages 196, 197), Memorial Ave. "A New England Colonial Village re-erected and restored through the generosity of Mrs. James J. Storrow of Boston. The village comprises a church, mansion, lawyer's office, tavern and store, Cape Cod cottage, farmhouse and a huge barn and outbuildings." Owned and operated by the Eastern States Exposition in its grounds. OPEN: daily 9 to 5, June to October. ADMISSION: 50 cents, children over twelve, 35 cents.

STURBRIDGE OLD STURBRIDGE VILLAGE, (Pages 218-220), on Highway No. 20 west of its junction with Highways 15 and 131. "Old Sturbridge Village portrays a New England country town as it might have appeared early in the 19th Century." Under the direction of Albert B. Wells and J. Cheney Wells the Village was begun in 1936. The mission of Old Sturbridge Village is to dramatize the struggle inherent in that early life of 150 years ago and the simple, primitive beauty that it produced. The Village is open daily from 10 a.m. to 4 p.m. during the months of June, July, August, and September. Guide service is provided through the exhibits. Special arrangements may be made for large groups and school age children. Admission fees and receipts from the sale of craftsmen's handiwork being used to defray the costs of operation.

SWAMPSCOTT HUMPHREY HOUSE, 99 Paradise Road. 17th Century house owned by the Swampscott Historical Society. OPEN: at all reasonable hours. EXHIBITS: gunstock corner posts, framed overhang with massive oak timbers, feathered pine panelling. No admission fee.

SWANSEA MARTIN HOUSE, (Page 153), corner Fall River Ave. and Short St. Built 1728 by John Martin. Owned by the Massachusetts Society of Colonial Dames of America. OPEN: week days and Sundays 10 to 6, June to November 1. EXHIBITS: old pewter, china, silver, furniture, cooking implements, clocks, samplers, portraits, etc. ADMISSION: 30 cents, children 15 cents.

TEMPLETON — NARRAGANSETT HISTORICAL BUILDING, (Page 234), facing Templeton Common. Built about 1810 by John W. Stiles, trader for Colonel Ephraim Stone, for a store. Restored 1934. Owned and operated by the Narragansett Historical Society, Inc. OPEN: Tuesday and Saturday, 2 to 5, from July 1 to October 15. Also the first Sunday of Summer months from 2 to 5. EXHIBITS: hand-pumped fire engine, tin peddler's cart, and a comprehensive exhibit of civil war relics and uniforms, period furniture. Also a weaving room with an old loom, spinning wheels and some of their products, and an old country store complete with Postoffice and a drug corner. Tea is served Saturday afternoons in the old-fashioned garden. No admission fee.

TOPSFIELD — PARSON CAPEN HOUSE, (Pages 100-102), Howlett St., just off the Village Common. Built 1683 by Reverend Joseph Capen. Restored 1913. Owned and operated by the Topsfield Historical Society. OPEN: week days 9 to 5, May 15 to October 15, Closed Sundays. EXHIBITS: 17th Century interiors. ADMISSION: 10 cents.

TOWNSEND HARBOR — CONANT HOUSE, Lunenberg Road. Built 1720. Reversion owned by the Society for the Preservation of New England Antiquities. OPEN: only by prior written appointment with Mrs. Leslie T. Stow, Townsend Harbor, Mass.

TOWNSEND HARBOR — SPAULDING COOPERAGE SHOP, Lunenberg Road. Built 1845. Owned and operated by the Society for the Preservation of New England Antiquities. OPEN: to visitors interested in local arts and crafts work, June to October.

TOWNSEND HARBOR — SPAULDING GRIST MILL, (Page 244), Lunenberg Road. Built about 1840. Owned and operated by the Society for the Preservation of New England Antiquities. OPEN: to visitors interested in local arts and crafts work.

WALTHAM — GORE PLACE, (Pages 223-226), Route 20 on the Watertown-Waltham town line. Built 1802-1804 by Governor Christopher Gore. Owned and operated by the Gore Place Society, Inc. OPEN: week days and Sundays, 10 to 5, the year round. Many rooms furnished in the style of the period. There are also a stable, coach house, farm cottage and extensive grounds. ADMISSION: 30 cents, children 15 cents.

WATERTOWN — ABRAHAM BROWNE, JR. HOUSE, (Pages 111, 112), 562 Main St. (Route 20). Built about 1690 by Abraham Browne, Jr. Addition built in 1720. Owned and operated by the Society for the Preservation of New England Antiquities. Mr. and Mrs. Ralph Burnham, custodians. OPEN: week days 2 to 5, the year round. EXHIBITS: 17th and 18th Century rooms. ADMISSION: 25 cents.

WATERTOWN — RICHARD DERBY'S McINTIRE-DESIGNED BARN, 562 Main St. Erected for Elias Haskett Derby. Owned and operated by the Society for the Preservation of New England Antiquities. Mr. and Mrs. Ralph Burnham, custodians. EXHIBITS: a good collection of horse-drawn vehicles. OPEN: only by special arrangement.

WENHAM — CLAFLIN-RICHARDS HOUSE, (Page 81). Main St., opposite the Village Green, (Route 1A). Built before 1664, probably by Robert MacClafflin. Owned and operated by the Wenham Historical Association. OPEN: week days 1:30 to 5, June to September 15. Sundays by appointment. EXHIBITS: doll museum of 1000 dolls, shoe shop with tools, barn with old implements. No admission fee to house.

WEST
NEWBURY

INDIAN HILL FARM, Indian Hill St. (follow Cherry Hill Nurseries signs from Newburyport Turnpike), Nucleus of house built about 1830. Many rooms added during lifetime of Major Ben Perley Poore. Owned and operated by the Society for the Preservation of New England Antiquities. OPEN: week days 10 to 5, during summer months. EXHIBITS: about 37 completely furnished rooms, some of which include architectural details from early houses, including the Province House, Boston. ADMISSION: 50 cents, school children 25 cents.

WEST
SPRINGFIELD

JOSIAH DAY HOUSE, (Page 168), 70 Park St., on the Town Green. Built 1754 by Josiah Day. Interior restored 1943. Owned and operated by the Ramapogue Historical Society. OPEN: Tuesday, Thursday and Saturday 9 to 6, except during the winter months. Closed Sundays. EXHIBITS: furniture, crockery, clothing, Colonial relics. ADMISSION: 10 cents.

WHITMAN

THE TOLL HOUSE, 362 Bedford St. Built 1709. Remodeled 1930. Owned and operated by Mr. and Mrs. Kenneth Wakefield. OPEN: daily from 12 to 9, the year round. EXHIBITS: ship staircase. The building was used as a toll house during the height of the whaling industry in New Bedford. Now an inn. No admission fee.

WINTHROP

DEANE WINTHROP HOUSE, (Page 60), 40 Shirley St. Built 1637 by Captain William Pierce. Occupied 1647-1703 by Deane Winthrop, younger son of Governor Winthrop. Owned and operated by the Winthrop Historical and Improvement Society. OPEN: Tuesday, Wednesday and Friday 2 to 5, the year round. Closed Sundays. EXHIBITS: pictures, relics and records of the house. ADMISSION: 10 cents, children 5 cents.

WOBURN

THE COUNT RUMFORD HOUSE, (Page 144), 90 Elm St., about two miles north of the town center. Built 1714 by Ebenezer Thompson, grandfather of Benjamin Thompson, who became Count Rumford. Owned and operated by the Rumford Historical Association. OPEN: daily, the year round. EXHIBITS: the "Rumford Roaster," cradle, portraits, period furniture, an English garden, etc. No admission fee.

WORCESTER

SALISBURY HOUSE, (Page 243), 61 Harvard St. Built about 1835 by Stephen Salisbury II. Remodeled 1909 and 1941. Owned and operated by the Worcester Chapter, American Red Cross. OPEN: the year round (except Sundays and Holidays), week days 9 to 5, Saturdays 9 to 12 noon. No admission fee.

YARMOUTHPORT

COLONEL JOHN THATCHER HOUSE, (Page 98), corner King's Highway and Thacher Lane. Original part built about 1680. Owned and operated by the Society for the Preservation of New England Antiquities. Miss Ethel Bailey, custodian. OPEN: week days 10 to 5, during the summer months. EXHIBITS: period furniture, etc. ADMISSION: 25 cents.

YARMOUTHPORT

WINSLOW CROCKER HOUSE, King's Highway. An 18th Century house owned by the Society for the Preservation of New England Antiquities. Miss Mary Thatcher, custodian. OPEN: only by appointment.

NEW HAMPSHIRE

EXETER

CINCINNATI HALL, (Page 150), Governor's Lane. Built 1721 by Nathaniel Ladd. Addition in 1775. Formerly the Ladd-Gilman house. Owned and operated by the Society of the Cincinnati in the State of New Hampshire. OPEN: Thursdays 2 to 4, the year round, upon application to caretaker. EXHIBITS: portraits, prints, documents, furniture, memorabilia of the Revolutionary period. No admission fee.

FRANKLIN   DANIEL WEBSTER BIRTHPLACE, (Page 198). Built 1782. Owned by the Webster Birthplace Association.

HANCOCK   THE JOHN HANCOCK HOUSE, Route 123. Built about 1793, restored 1940. Owned and operated by Mr. and Mrs. William D. Roche. For more than 150 years an inn along the Milford-Hancock turnpike. OPEN: year round at reasonable hours. EXHIBITS: unique wall paintings by an itinerant painter. No admission fee.

HANCOCK   THE HISTORICAL BUILDING, (Page 232). Built about 1810. Owned and operated by the Hancock Historical Society. OPEN: June to September. No admission fee.

HENNIKER   OCEAN BORN MARY HOUSE (Page 178), located in the hills about three miles from the town. Well marked with signs. Built about 1760. OPEN: during the summer months upon application. A picturesque legend has come down concerning the early inhabitants of this house.

PETERBOROUGH   "BLEAKHOUSE," on the Wilton Road at Pine St., 1 mile south of the town. Built 1770-1790 by John White. Remodeled 1870-1880. Owned by the Society for the Preservation of New England Antiquities. Open the year round as a guest house.

PORTSMOUTH   DAVENPORT HOUSE, 321 State St.. Built 1758 by Mrs. Charles Treadwell. Owned by the Y.W.C.A. of Portsmouth. EXHIBITS: interesting interior woodwork. OPEN: daily 8 a.m. to 11 p.m. Closed Sunday at mid-day. No admission fee.

PORTSMOUTH   RICHARD JACKSON HOUSE, (Page 83), Jackson Hill St. Christian Shore, just off Route 4 about 1/2 mile from the railway station. Built 1664 by Richard Jackson. Extensions made on three different occasions. Owned and operated by the Society for the Preservation of New England Antiquities. Mr. and Mrs. Harry M. S. Harlow, custodians. OPEN: 11 to 5, June 18 to September 25. Exhibits of architectural interest. ADMISSION: 15 cents.

PORTSMOUTH   JOHN PAUL JONES HOUSE, (Page 171), 45 Middle St. Built 1758 by Captain Gregory Purcell. Owned and operated by the Portsmouth Historical Society. EXHIBITS: Revolutionary relics, etc.

PORTSMOUTH   TOBIAS LEAR HOUSE, (Page 160), Hunking St., near the Wentworth-Gardner House. Built about 1740 by Tobias Lear, 3rd of the name, and secretary to George Washington. Owned by Mr. Arthur Dewing. Operated by the Society for the Preservation of New England Antiquities. OPEN: by appointment.

PORTSMOUTH   MOFFATT-LADD HOUSE, 35 Market St., (Pages 182, 183). Built 1763 by John Moffatt. Leased and operated by the National Society of the Colonial Dames of America in the State of New Hampshire. OPEN: week days 10 to 5, June to October. Closed Sundays. EXHIBITS: pewter, old furniture, silver, portraits, china, bedspreads, etc. Grinling Gibbons carving in mantel-pieces, fine old wall paper, Colonial garden, counting house, etc. ADMISSION: 50 cents, children 25 cents.

PORTSMOUTH   THE NUTTER HOUSE, (Page 239), 386 Court St. Built about 1820. Owned and operated by the Thomas Bailey Aldrich Memorial. OPEN: week days 10 to 5, from latter part of June until after Labor Day. Closed Sundays. EXHIBITS: books, autographs and memorabilia of Thomas Bailey Aldrich. ADMISSION: 25 cents.

PORTSMOUTH   WARNER HOUSE, (Page 147), Daniels and Chapel Sts. Built 1718 by Captain Archibald MacPhaedris. Owned and operated by the Warner House Association. OPEN: week days 10 to 5, June 15 to September 15. Closed Sundays. EXHIBITS: furniture and portraits. ADMISSION: 30 cents, children free.

PORTSMOUTH   WENTWORTH-GARDNER HOUSE, (Pages 173-175), Gardner and Mechanic Sts. Built 1760. Owned by the Metropolitan Museum of Art. Administered by the Society for the Preservation of New England Antiquities. OPEN: week days 10 to 5:30, May to November. Sundays by appointment. ADMISSION: 25 cents, children under 5 free.

SHARON   LAWS HOUSE, New Ipswich Road, (Route 123). Built about 1800. Owned and operated by the Society for the Preservation of New England Antiquities. The house is a part of the Sharon Arts Center, a project sponsored by Mr. William L. Young. OPEN: by appointment.

RHODE ISLAND

ANTHONY   NATHANAEL GREENE HOMESTEAD, (Page 190), 20 Taft St. Built 1770 by Nathanael Greene. Interior restored 1919. Owned and operated by the Nathanael Greene Homestead Association. OPEN: by appointment. EXHIBITS: furnishings and relics of the period of 1770.

KINGSTON   HELME HOUSE, Kingstowne Road(Route 138). Built 1802 by John T. Nichols and remodeled in 1933. Owned and operated by the South County Art Association. OPEN: by appointment. No admission fee.

LINCOLN   ELEAZER ARNOLD HOUSE, (Page 108), Great Road, near Saylesville. Built about 1687 by Eleazer Arnold. Owned and operated by the Society for the Preservation of New England Antiquities. OPEN: by appointment. See custodian in neighboring house. EXHIBITS: largest fireplace in the state. ADMISSION: 15 cents.

MIDDLETOWN   WHITEHALL, (Page 153), Berkeley Ave. Built 1729 by the philosopher George Berkeley, Dean of Londonderry and Bishop of Cloyne, Ireland. Remodeled 1897 and 1936. Owned by Yale University. Leased and operated by the National Society of Colonial Dames in the State of Rhode Island. OPEN: July and August, other times by appointment. EXHIBITS: architecture and floor plan of the house, original woodwork, tiles, engravings and books. ADMISSION: 25 cents.

NEWPORT   MAWDSLEY-GARDNER-WATSON-PITMAN HOUSE, 228 Spring St. Built about 1700. Owned and operated by the Society for the Preservation of New England Antiquities. Miss Alice C. Banning, custodian. Certain rooms are shown at reasonable hours. ADMISSION: 25 cents.

NEWPORT   VERNON HOUSE, 46 Clarke St. Built about 1758 by Metcalf Bowler. Owned and operated by the Family Welfare Society of Newport. OPEN: Monday through Friday, 9 to 5, the year round. EXHIBITS: panelled room, hall, stairway, Chinese murals in northwest room. The building was used as headquarters of General de Rochambeau. No admission fee.

NEWPORT   WANTON-LYMAN-HAZARD HOUSE, (Page 91), 17 Broadway, corner Stone St. Built about 1675. Restored 1929. Owned and operated by the Newport Historical Society. OPEN: Tuesday through Saturday 2:30 to 5:30, during summer months. Sundays 3 to 5 (subject to change), other times by appointment. EXHIBITS: antiques, glass, fans, laces, and a fully furnished period kitchen. This was the scene of the Stamp Tax riot in 1765. ADMISSION: 25 cents, Servicemen and small children free.

NORTH
KINGSTOWN

BIRTHPLACE OF GILBERT STUART, (Page 164), Hammond Hill Road, midway between Post Road and Tower Hill Road, (well marked with signs). Built about 1750, probably by Edward Cole and Dr. Thomas Moffat. Owned and operated by the Gilbert Stuart Memorial, Inc. OPEN: week days and Sundays, 9 to 6, the year round. EXHIBITS: 18th Century snuff mill, fireplaces, grist mill and relics of the period. ADMISSION: 25 cents, school children free.

PAWTUCKET

DAGGETT HOUSE, (Page 69), Slater Park. Original part said to date from 1644. Repaired 1905. Owned by the City of Pawtucket. Maintained by the Pawtucket Chapter, Daughters of the American Revolution. OPEN: by appointment with members of the Pawtucket Chapter, D.A.R. EXHIBITS: antique furniture, china, glassware, etc. ADMISSION: 25 cents, children 15 cents.

PROVIDENCE

JOHN BROWN HOUSE, (Pages 201, 202), 52 Power St. Built in 1786 by John Brown, designed by Joseph Brown. Owned and operated by the Rhode Island Historical Society. OPEN: Monday through Friday 9 to 5, Tuesday evening 7 to 9, Sunday 3 to 5, the year round. The house contains a library and a museum of Rhode Island material. No admission fee.

PROVIDENCE

CARRINGTON HOUSE, (Page 236), 66 Williams St. Built about 1810. Owned and operated by the Rhode Island School of Design. OPEN: week days, except Monday, 1 to 5, Sundays 1 to 5, April through November. EXHIBITS: original wall papers, Lowestoft china, early 19th Century furniture, etc. No admission fee.

PROVIDENCE

ESEK HOPKINS HOUSE, (Page 171), 97 Admiral St., near a playing field, (Route 146). Original two-story gambrel-roof section built in 1756. Owned and operated by the Park Department, City of Providence. OPEN: week days 1 to 5, the year round. Closed Sundays and on days when meetings are held. This was the home of the first Commander-in-Chief of the American Navy. No admission fee.

PROVIDENCE

STEPHEN HOPKINS HOUSE, (Page 143), corner of Hopkins and Benefit Sts. Built prior to 1708 by John Field Jr. Remodeled 1741. Owned and operated by the National Society of Colonial Dames in the State of Rhode Island. OPEN: Tuesday and Thursday, 2 to 4, the year round. EXHIBITS: original documents, furniture, glassware and china. No admission fee.

PROVIDENCE

BETSEY WILLIAMS COTTAGE, (Page 190), Williams Park. Built 1773 by Nathaniel Williams for his son James, father of Betsey Williams. Owned and operated by the City of Providence, Park Department. OPEN: week days (except Thursday) 9 to 5, Sunday 1 to 5, the year round EXHIBITS: furniture and utensils used by Betsey Williams. No admission fee.

VERMONT

BROWNINGTON

OLD STONE HOUSE. Built about 1828 by Alexander Twilight. Owned and operated by the Orleans County Historical Society. OPEN: week days and Sundays, 9 to dusk, May to October. EXHIBITS: early furniture, china, glass, implements, books, etc. ADMISSION: 50 cents for parties.

BURLINGTON

GRASSMOUNT, (Page 230), 411 Main St. Built 1804 by Captain Thaddeus Tuttle. Owned by the University of Vermont. Now used as women's dormitory. OPEN: when students are not in residence, by request to the Superintendent of Buildings and Grounds, Waterman Building. No admission fee.

CALAIS

KENT TAVERN AND COUNTRY STORE FARMER'S MU-SEUM, Kents Corners. Built in 1837 by Addiel Kent. Owned and operated by the Vermont Historical Society. OPEN: daily, June through September. EXHIBITS: farmer's museum, tools and implements and a country store. No admission fee.

FERRISBURG

"ROKEBY," (Page 200), on Route 7, one mile north of Ferrisburg Center. Original part built before 1784. Main part built 1812 by Thomas Robinson. Owned and operated by Rowland T. and Elizabeth N. Robinson. OPEN: week days and Sundays, anytime after 9 a.m., May 1 to October 1. EXHIBITS: early American furnishings, intimate surroundings of Rowland Evans Robinson, artist and author. ADMISSION: 25 cents, children free.

GRAFTON

THE TAVERN, Main St. Built about 1835. Remodeled in 1865 by Francis and Harland Phelps. Owned and operated by Mr. and Mrs. Clarence Detemus. OPEN: July and August. No admission fee.

MIDDLEBURY

MIDDLEBURY COMMUNITY HOUSE (formerly Battell House). Built 1815. Owned by Horatio Seymour and operated by the Middlebury Community House Corporation. OPEN: week days (except Monday) 1 to 5, 7 to 9, the year round. Sundays 10:45 to 12. EXHIBITS: circular stairway, old stove and oven in basement kitchen. No admission fee.

MIDDLEBURY

SHELDON MUSEUM, Main St. opposite Illsley Library. Built 1829 by Dr. Eben Warner Judd and Lebbeus Harris, his son-in-law. Owned and operated by the Sheldon Art Museum, Archaeological and Historical Society, Inc. OPEN: week days 10 to 12, 2 to 5. Sundays 2 to 5, June 15 to September 15. EXHIBITS: a museum collection of early America of all sorts. ADMISSION: 25 cents, children 10 cents.

WEST ADDISON

GENERAL JOHN STRONG HOUSE. Built 1871. Owned and operated by the State Daughters of the American Revolution. Route 17. Open to the public the year round.

WESTON

FARRAR-MANSUR HOUSE, north end of Western Common. Built in 1787 by Captain Oliver Farrar. Owned and operated by the Weston Community Club. OPEN: week days 10 to 5, Sundays 2 to 5, from June to December. EXHIBITS: murals by contemporary American painters. The building is completely furnished with antiques, showing how an old tavern once looked. No admission fee.

WINDSOR

OLD CONSTITUTION HOUSE, (Page 187), 14 North Main St. Built about 1768. Restored 1912. Owned and operated by the Old Constitution House Association. OPEN: week days and Sundays, May 1 to November 1. EXHIBITS: old furniture, pictures, chamfered beams, etc. No admission fee. Now a tea room.

WOODSTOCK

DANA HOUSE, Elm Street. Built 1807 by Charles Dana. Owned by The Woodstock Historical Society, Inc. OPEN: July through October, 9 to 12, 1:30 to 5. EXHIBITS: antiques, furniture, old household and farm implements, portraits and a fine stone kitchen fireplace. No admission fee.

Open House in New England

Abraham Browne, Jr. House, Watertown, Mass.

III

Seventeenth Century Houses

New England's first settlement, of course, was in Plymouth. The original hillside thoroughfare, Leyden Street, still exists, but with it there is no trace of the crude huts which comprised the first settlement. The "log cabin myth" has been pretty well disproven by archaeologists, and Leyden Street was sparsely lined with quite a different type of habitation. It is fortunate, therefore, that a replica of "The settlement in the wilderness that was Salem in 1630" has been erected. With the aid of antiquarians, the city has reconstructed the sod-roofed dug-outs, the bark covered wigwams and the pine cottages, roofed with thatch, which sheltered the first intrepid settlers. Here is the one-room house with the steep roof and a dark attic which served as a dormitory for surplus offspring (Pages 55-56). The "Governor's fayre house" reproduces the larger two-room type, built around a massive chimney. The crude furnishings of those hardy days, the utensils for kitchen, farm, forge and buttery, all are displayed. Even the pillory and stocks stand at the village crossroads. This graphic picture of home life in New England 300 years ago has been enlarged by the addition of the Ruck House, perhaps the oldest in Salem (built 1651), which was dismembered to make way for the new Postoffice. Just before the Revolution, John Singleton Copley lived in this house while painting portraits of the more opulent citizens of the town. A full sized model of Governor Winthrop's flagship, the "Arbella," is moored in the village, giving a salty picture of the hazards and romance of sailing a merchant ship in the early 17th Century.

"Aptucxet" is another replica, built after the most careful research, upon the original foundations of the first trading post on Cape Cod (Page 56). For years the English merchants and the Dutch from New Amsterdam came here to trade with the Plymouth Colonists, thus making it one of the earliest pillars of American commerce. It was the first organized business in New England, and possibly in the country. Again the steep roof, this time covered with extremely wide, hand-hewn shingles, is in evidence.

The famous Fairbanks House (Pages 57, 58) in Dedham, built in 1636 with oak timbers brought from England, gives a picture which is startling in its authenticity. It may well be the oldest frame house in America, and few would deny that its harmonious, rambling lines make it one of the most picturesque. The middle portion with the steep roof was obviously the original structure. A gambrel-roofed ell was added at the east about 1648. It is still in a splendid state of preservation, and its oak frame is as solid as rock. One family, and only one, has lived in the house since it was built by the original Jonathan Fairbanks. In 312 years it has never been deeded or mortgaged, a house of multiple distinctions indeed.

The nucleus of the Hartwell House, in Lincoln, Mass., may be almost as ancient, but it is concealed by a fine old weathered facade of later date (Page 59). This house was well placed to witness the dramatic days of the Revolution, since the British tramped past it on the way to Concord on that fateful April day in 1775. During the retreat, the Red Coats were in too much of a hurry to burn it, but one of them thrust his musket through a window as a parting gesture. In recent years the Hartwell Farm has been converted into a rural restaurant of considerable prestige, and its historical interest is now rivaled by its gastronomic appeal.

A good deal of restoration hides the antiquity of the Deane Winthrop House (Page 60), which was built by one of the first trans-Atlantic sea captains, and occupied by the son of Governor Winthrop. It can surely lay claim, however, to being one of the first "salt-box" houses.

One of the members of Roger Conant's party of Salem settlers was John Balch, of Somersetshire, who settled on Cape Ann in 1624, very much at the dawn of New England. After travelling back to England to take himself a bride, he returned to Salem, and upon being given a grant of land, built a small, steep-roofed house in 1638 (Pages 60-62). This original fragment is probably the two-gabled corner, and represents but about one-fifth of the present structure. The atmosphere is strongly English. John Balch may well have employed carpenters who had English training to build his Beverly home.

Meantime early settlements were springing up along the Connecticut River, Windsor being one of the first. The townspeople were apprehensive of the

Indians, and at the outbreak of the Pequot War their houses were surrounded by ditches and high palisades of stakes. It was perhaps a wise precaution, since the town was not attacked. The old Fyler House (Page 62) was thus protected. Three small rooms, one of which was Windsor's first Postoffice, an attic and a lean-to constituted the original house. Palisado Avenue still exists in Windsor.

The town of Guilford, Conn., was founded by the Rev. Henry Whitfield, who built a stone house there, overlooking Long Island Sound, in 1639. It was more than a commodious dwelling, it was the town's fort and meeting house (Page 63). It is the oldest stone house now standing in New England. The stone came from a ledge nearby, and was carried to the building site, according to tradition, by friendly Menuncatuck Indians. The house was burned out in the 19th Century and rebuilt in the style of that time. A comprehensive restoration has recently taken place with the help of WPA funds, with the result that the Whitfield House and its massive chimneys have been restored to the original state. It is the outstanding monument in this old town, but not the only one, for Guilford has at least a hundred houses which antedate the Revolution. Stone houses were plentiful along the Connecticut and Rhode Island shore but rare elsewhere. Structurally they differed from the frame houses in one important way—the chimneys were built in the end walls and not in the center of the house. The Reverend Whitfield, after getting Guilford well established as a town, returned to England where he died, and was buried in Winchester Cathedral.

As successors to the first crude dwellings, the early settlers did not build larger and slightly *less* crude houses. It comes as a surprise to learn that they built instead English manor houses of a pronounced medieval character. The explanation is simple enough. The first craftsmen imported from England brought over their traditional building habits and constructed houses which bore an amazing similarity to the middle class manors in the mother country. The steep roofs, ornamental overhangs, leaded windows and pilastered chimneys were some of the obvious features which could have been duplicated in countless English towns. The Whipple House in Ipswich (Pages 64, 65) is a good illustration. This house is architecturally significant as one of the first to boast a hewn end overhang. This feature, which lent a pleasing touch to many an English manor house, occurs on the gable end of the house. Projections of the upper floors are made possible by the use of unusually wide vertical supports, which are left broad at the top and hewn away below, thus providing the framework for an overhang. From a small beginning this house underwent many additions, as did the Whipple families who grew up in it. Its original triple sashes have been restored, but not with the lead muntins.

Along with Guilford, Ipswich is one of those rare communities which still possess unrestored 17th Century houses in comparative abundance. It won't be possible to make this statement a few years from now for, one by one, these ancient treasures are being bought up and restored by appreciative, antiquarian-minded home seekers. Not many of them are open to visitors, but one of them not only welcomes the stranger, but provides him with very fine food and drink during the summer months. This is the venerable Wooden Hart House, built in 1640 (Page 65). It is well known to visitors who have seen the American Wing of the Metropolitan Museum of Art in New York, for two of its rooms have been transplanted there, and a third one has been reproduced. Copies have replaced the originals in the Hart House, and none of the early atmosphere is lost.

The first frame house in Haverhill was built by the Reverend John Ward about 1645 in a sylvan spot overlooking the Merrimac River. The little gambrel-roofed structure (Page 66) began as a one room house. Later a west room and an upper story were added. It stands on its original spot, serene and untroubled by the industrial hub-bub which has invaded nearby acres, and furnished in a style befitting the town's first minister.

An unforgettable experience is in store for the inquiring visitor who seeks out the Old Ironworks House in Saugus (Page 67) for this is perhaps the most striking example of an English manor house adapted to the New England countryside. Directly across the road from this startling medieval structure was the birthplace of the iron industry in America. In 1642 the first crude forge was established in this little valley. Saugus then bore the appropriate name of Hammersmith, an idyllic predecessor to Pittsburgh, Youngstown and Gary. This house was built for Richard Leader, manager of the plant. According to tradition the first designs for the Pine Tree and Oak Tree shillings were made in this house. The first fire engine in America is said to have come from the plant, along with countless anchors, cranes, and kettles. A congenial iron worker still presides over the place and operates a forge in the smaller building at the right, making replicas of all sorts of early ironwork from hinges to weather vanes. The ancient house has undergone extensive restoration, some of which, particularly on the exterior, is a bit imaginative. The interiors show restraint and keen understanding on the part of the restorers, and recent additions of fine 17th Century pieces make the house a noteworthy specimen indeed.

The Emerson-Howard House in Ipswich is a fine example of the hewn overhang central chimney type, with two large rooms on either side on both floors (Pages 68, 69). At one time each of these four rooms was partitioned into three smaller rooms, making twelve in all, as a solution to the large family problem. The street names in Ipswich have a certain fascination. The Emerson-Howard House is now on Turkey Hill Road, which at one time was a mere cow-path called Wood's Lane, leading to Labor-in-Vain Fields.

The Daggett House, set in the beautiful landscaping of Slater Park, in Pawtucket (Page 69), is so well kept that it does not look its years. The original core, however, is supposed to be nearly three centuries old.

The James Blake House in Dorchester (Page 70), dating from 1648, is a good example of the steep-roofed two-and-a-half story cottage which flourished in the Boston area in those primitive days.

The Macy-Colby House in Amesbury (Page 70) is a smaller variation of the same persistent theme: central chimney, long sloping roof, two rooms and a hallway. Its original builder, Thomas Macy, had to leave Amesbury in a hurry when he was accused of the crime of harboring Quakers in his house during a storm. With his wife and children he fled in a light wherry, rowed to Nantucket, built a log cabin and began life anew. Plenty of his descendents are still on Nantucket Island. He is the hero of John Greenleaf Whittier's poem, "The Exiles," based on this story.

The oldest house in Boston (Page 71), might have been lifted intact out of an English town. It is a good example of "framed" or structural overhang, being supported by projecting horizontal beams instead of wide upright members hewn away at the base. The architectural side of this house is overshadowed by the fact that Paul Revere lived here for thirty years, enough to lend distinction to any house. It was his home at the time of his memorable midnight ride. The house consists of four rooms and an attic, admirably furnished and well stocked with Revere memorabilia. The chattering army of Italian urchins which greets the visitor in this crowded corner of North Square will probably recall sight-seeing days in Europe more than any spot in New England.

Few houses give a better picture of the intimate home life of the 17th century than the Tristram Coffin House in Newbury (Pages 72-74). It is not difficult to picture the pioneer family clustered about this hearth, its sole source of heat and cooking. Several pots, hung by adjustable trammels, could simmer over the log fire at once. A revolving spit, imported from Europe, would turn slowly while fat sputtered from a roasting fowl. A vaulted brick oven was an integral part of the chimney. The good housewife would fill the oven with hot coals, or else build a fire of birchwood inside. When the bricks had stored up enough heat, she would scrape out the embers, give the oven a good dusting and put in her corn bread or Indian pudding or beans. There were grills which could be pushed over the hot coals, long-handled frying pans and an infinite assortment of ladles and skewers. A spinning wheel was a vital part of the scene, which must have been a soul-warming one. The Coffin House started as a modest cottage, which is now the rear ell. But Tristram and Judith Coffin had ten children, and the larger east end (Page 72) was needed to shelter them. The house remained in the Coffin family until 1929 when it was given by the last owner to the Society for the Preservation of New England Antiquities. One of its most distinguished occupants was Joshua Coffin, historian and teacher of Whittier.

Of the several old taverns now open to the public, few have more fascination than the Old Ordinary (Page 74) in the delightful town of Hingham. One is transported back a century or two by the sight of its ancient public rooms, quite unchanged since the earliest stagecoach days. Many additions have made the outside appearance a bit confused.

The exterior of the "Scotch"-Boardman House in Saugus, however, gives about as perfect and un-retouched a picture of a 17th Century house as can be found in New England. The same simple central-chimney plan can be read on its countenance (Pages 75, 76). Much of the original sheathing, casements and woodwork remains. Its pilastered brick chimney is a treasure. This house is perhaps the first to have documents proving its age. These show that it was built in 1651 as quarters for Scotch prisoners who were captured in the Battle of Dunbar and shipped to New England, there to labor in the Saugus iron works. They were estimable prisoners of war, and soon became absorbed into the community. The original boundary line between Lynn and Boston once ran through the middle of the front door of this house, and for years the letters B and L were emblazoned on the respective door panels.

Said to be the only house standing which was actually occupied by *Mayflower* Pilgrims, the John Alden House in Duxbury (Page 76), has never left the Alden family. John and Priscilla Alden lived here about twelve years, and both died in the house. Their memory overshadows the architectural virtues of the place, which are many.

The oldest public building in America, according to some claims, is the Old Gaol, in York, Maine, a low, gambrel-roofed structure built in 1653, which long served as a Courthouse for York County. Painted a dark red and lost in abundant foliage, it is a difficult subject to photograph, but a gratifying one to visit. Its collection of Colonial furniture and costumes makes it a most significant small museum (Page 77). No change has been made in the original building.

One of the most venerable houses in Plymouth can sometimes put up an over-night guest or two. This is the trim gambrel-roofed Kendall Holmes House, dating from 1653 (Page 77). Its great central chimney gives it distinction from without, and exudes New England hospitality within. In addition it can claim a charming garden, bright with roses, phlox and hollyhocks.

Cambridge's most venerable house (Page 78) is a joy to behold. Its old chimney, embellished by brick pilasters and a crudely lettered "1657," exists in its entirety. Its framework is in splendid shape, as the fine old carved and chamfered beams will testify. This was one of the first acquisitions of the Society for the Preservation of New England Antiquities, that timely and public-spirited organization which has rescued so many worthwhile monuments about to disappear. Lacking a governmental agency such as the French Ministère des Beaux Arts which can classify a noteworthy structure as a "monument historique" and thus preserve it, New England is fortunate indeed in having a vigilant and unselfish society such as this to arouse public opinion and to undertake the thankless task of raising funds to preserve its antiquities. The Society is constantly assuming new responsibilities and acquiring added properties, many of which appear in the present edition for the first time.

The oldest house in Northampton (Page 79) was the homestead of a true pioneer, Joseph Parsons. A fur trader and explorer, he sailed from England in 1636, was one of the founders of Springfield, and later became the first settler of Northampton in 1654. His wife, Mary Bliss, was accused of being a witch and held in jail in Boston for three months awaiting trial. She defended herself well at the trial, and was acquitted. Joseph Parsons, first of his family in America, was proud of being "Cornet of the Hampshire Troop of Horse." His pleasant old homestead is now a veritable museum of early relics.

When James Babson, barrel maker, made himself a stone cooperage shop in the wilds of Cape Ann in 1659, he built substantially, and well. His shop still stands, furnished with old cooperage tools, and very well groomed after a recent restoration (Page 79). In this shop, which may well have been the first of its kind in America, James Babson was busy making barrels to ship dried codfish from the nearby beaches to England.

The "salt-box" type of house is one of New England's conspicuous contributions to domestic architecture. It is achieved, of course, by the simple expedient of carrying the rear roof closer to the ground, thus creating a "lean-to" with added space. Often another fireplace was built onto the chimney stack at the same time, to heat the new quarters. A very fine Connecticut salt-box is the Hyland House, in historic Guilford (Page 80). This overhang is finely hewn, with girts beautifully chamfered and supported by flat wooden corbels. The interior of the house, with the original stone chimney, fine old staircase and much ancient woodwork, is one of the least changed in the state. Ebenezer Parmelee, a grandson of the original builder, was a noted clockmaker, and built in this house the first town clock in America. It is now on exhibit in the Whitfield State Historical Museum. In 1916 the house was about to be torn down when Governor Woodruff intervened with only a week to spare. As a result the Dorothy Whitfield Society took the title.

The architectural treasures of Salem have been preserved due to the combined vigilance and energy of the municipality, numerous civic organizations and many individuals. The City of Salem is responsible for the rescue and restoration of the celebrated Witch House (Page 80). This was the home of Jonathan Corwin, one of the judges at the witchcraft trials. It seems probable that some of the preliminary hearings were held in this house. The steep Elizabethan gables, pilastered chimney and leaded panes all point to the unquestioned antiquity of the house, which has only recently been opened to visitors. Some of Salem's most charming young ladies, dressed in the severe costumes of the times, show visitors through the well authenticated rooms.

The Stanley-Whitman House in Farmington, Conn. (Page 82) is a rather elaborate "salt-box" with a fine structural overhang and some of the handhewn "drops" still in place. The overhang had some practical value in England, but on these shores it seems to have been used for its decorative value only. It is true that they were supposed to have shot at the Indians through a hole in this very overhang on the Stanley-Whitman house, but it could not have been a very efficacious defense. At one time it was thought that the overhang might be used to provide openings through which boiling water could be poured on the attackers, in true medieval fashion. The flaw in this reasoning is that the other three sides of the house usually had no overhang, making it three quarters vulnerable. And the Indians were not stupid! In a rainy English village the overhang might serve as a timely shelter, but it hardly sufficed in the blizzards of New England. So it appears that it was used by builders whose trained eyes were pleased by its picturesque qualities, and for no other reason.

Another salt-box farmhouse had the double distinction of being the home of one President of the United States and the birthplace of another. This is the John Quincy Adams Birthplace in Quincy (Page 82). The early law office of John Adams was in one room of this house, and here he wrote the Constitution of Massachusetts. The surfaces of the old house are now covered with red painted clapboards, but underneath them the outer walls are filled with brick, in the ancient tradition.

A splendid opportunity to study early timberwork is provided by the Claflin-Richards House in Wenham (Page 81). It contains several early ogee curved braces which, while common in England, are practically unknown in this country, and other bits of detail and woodwork which make it entirely unique. As if this were not enough, the house also boasts an extraordinary doll museum.

The Thomas Lee House in East Lyme (Page 81) is close to being the perfect salt-box externally and its interiors, medieval in character, are fascinating. From an archaeological point of view it is a Chinese puzzle. Although it faces North now (a rarity in itself), it apparently faced South in its original state before enlargements began. Fifteen children in a family (such was the record of Thomas Lee, Jr.), can cause a lot of juxtaposition in a house!

Of about the same age is the Richard Jackson house in Portsmouth (Page 83), a fine and exceedingly quaint (the only time this word appears in this book!) example of a fisherman's home in the 17th Century. The lines of this house would warm the heart of an artist, largely because of its phenomenally low lean-to, which extends practically to the ground. The primitive interior woodwork in the Richard Jackson House is truly extraordinary, and it is one of the most visited of Portsmouth's many open houses.

Two *Mayflower* passengers, John Howland and his wife Elizabeth, have often crossed the threshold of one old Plymouth house which welcomes summer visitors. This is the Jabez Howland House, recently restored with gratifying good taste and accuracy. When orginally built in 1666 by Jacob Mitchell, who was later killed by the Indians, it consisted of one large room with an immense chimney, and a staircase leading to the second floor and attic. Jabez Howland, son of John Howland, bought the house in 1667 and constructed a westerly wing for the use of his parents. Here Pilgrim John lived until his death in 1672. Among the many curiosities and relics to be seen in this house is an early brick showing the imprint of a wolf's foot (Page 84).

Three houses of extraordinary interest have been gathered together in the restful grounds of the House of Seven Gables, in Salem. One of them is the steep-roofed Turner-Ingersoll House (Pages 85, 86), which is apparently the house Nathaniel Hawthorne had in mind when selecting a name for his great romance. At all events, this house has been known as the House of Seven

Gables ever since. Hawthorne was a frequent visitor to the house, one of the few men permitted to cross the threshold by his spinster cousin, Miss Susan Ingersoll. The house is almost Elizabethan in character, with weathered clapboards, a fine overhang and a handsomely furnished interior which boasts, among other things, a secret staircase. The Hathaway House (Page 87), is another member of the quiet group at the water's edge. This was formerly known as the Old Bakery, and was about to be torn down in 1911 when rescued by Miss Caroline O. Emmerton and moved to the present site. It is an amazingly authentic fragment of medieval England. The beams in the house are cut with characteristic West of England carving, and were probably brought from there. Parts of the Hathaway house have been converted into guest rooms. The Hathaway Bakery, in modern form, still thrives. Third in the group is the Retire Beckett House, one of the few surviving examples of the structural overhang (Page 88). The Becketts were a family of shipbuilders, extending through five generations. The house is now filled with a fine collection of antiques, which are for sale. The gardens of the House of Seven Gables are exquisite, located on the shore where the Marblehead Ferry used to land years ago. A more reposeful spot for lunch or a cup of tea on a quiet summer's day would be hard to find. Most visitors leave the place in a mood of enchantment. All profits from the House of Seven Gables group are used for social welfare work in this district of Salem.

Though not particularly beautiful, the Eels-Stowe House in Milford (Page 88), is interesting to archaeologists. The wide plaster cove which extends across the cornice and beneath the projecting gables is a rare and unique feature. When, in the winter of 1777, a shipload of sick American prisoners were landed in Milford from a British prison ship, this house was converted into a hospital for them. Captain Stephen Stowe, who married Miss Freelove Baldwin, grand-daughter of the original builder, owned the house at this time and served as a voluntary nurse. Unhappily smallpox broke out, and a half hundred of the prisoners and their valiant host died.

The life story of the Swett-Ilsley House in Old Newbury, could it be told, would be a fascinating one (Page 89). Beginning as the primitive two-room home of an early settler, it gradually expanded into a family mansion and then was adapted as a tavern, a printing office, chocolate works and tallow chandlery. Its ancient Tap Room, with a tremendous ten-foot fireplace, has long since ceased to echo with raucous laughter. During the summer months it now serves as a very proper and choice tea room. The husky summer beams and much of the original panelling is still to be seen.

In the gracious old town of Rowley is a very sketchable farm group, marred only by the modern touch of a telephone wire. This is the Chaplin-Clarke-Williams House (Page 90) whose two successive overhangs lend a picturesque touch. Its long sloping roof almost touches the ground on the western end.

The earliest Bradford house extant is the old shingled salt-box on Pages 90 and 91. It is furnished very much as it was in the days when Major John

Bradford, grandson of Governor William Bradford of the *Mayflower,* brought his bride there. She was Mercy Warren, grand-daughter of Richard Warren, also of the *Mayflower,* and here they lived for "neare 62 year." Governor Bradford's manuscript "Of Plimouth Plantation" was kept in this old house for many years. The house was later the home of Colonel Joseph Sampson, of Revolutionary fame, and after the Irish immigration, it was the scene of the first Roman Catholic Mass celebrated in the vicinity. The house was partially burned in King Philip's War.

An ancient pilastered chimney gives a clue to the antiquity of the Wanton-Lyman-Hazard House (Page 91), in Newport, R. I. The facade is more·in the 18th Century tradition. A typical end-chimney kitchen was added about 1700. It is now fully furnished, constituting a culinary museum of great charm. This house was scene of a Stamp Tax riot in 1765, and French officers were entertained extensively here during the Revolutionary War.

At the close of King Philip's War, the Old Fort on Burial Hill, Plymouth, was abandoned. Sergeant William Harlow, a selectman and person of importance in the town used the timbers from the dismantled fort to construct one of the first wooden gambrel-roofed houses (Page 92). During the summer months, demonstrations of the early household arts are given in the Harlow House. A Pilgrim maid in costume carries out the process of preparing flax, spinning, weaving on a 200-year old loom, dyeing, cooking and candle-making, thus giving an intimate picture of the vigorous daily life of the housewife in days long before vacuum cleaners and electric stoves.

The traditional central chimney plan takes on more ample proportions with the Platts-Bradstreet House in Rowley (Page 93) and the four-room plan is definitely in the offing. The house was built some time before 1677 by Samuel Platts on land granted to William Bellingham, brother of an early Governor of the Massachusetts Bay Colony. A lean-to was added shortly after 1700. A small 19th Century shoe shop, completely fitted with benches and tools, now adjoins the house, and is shown during the summer months.

On the outskirts of Danvers is a noble old farmhouse which recalls the dark days of Salem witchcraft delusion of 1692. It is the Rebecca Nurse House, from whose fireside Rebecca Nurse, an estimable and courageous woman, mother of nine children, was dragged to the gallows, accused of being a witch. Nearby is her grave and a monument with an inscription composed by the poet Whittier. The old rooms of this house, with low, beamed ceilings and wall coverings of vertical planks, are almost uncanny in their 17th Century atmosphere (Pages 94, 95).

Probably the oldest brick building in New England is the Peter Tufts House in Medford (Page 96) which was built about 1678. Medford was long known for its brick kilns. In a desire to lessen the height of the steep roof, the top timbers were truncated, thus originating one of the first examples of gambrel roof in this country. The name "gambrel roof" is supposedly derived from its similarity to a gambrel or hock of a horse. Inside the Tufts House will be found exposed some superb oak beams and a part of the original staircase. The brick entrance porch is a none too happy addition of recent years.

The James Putnam House in Danvers (Page 96), belongs more to the period of 1715 than 1680, when its original core was built. Here is an early example of the central-hall type of structure, with two rooms on either side, each heated by a fireplace. The entrance portal is more impressive than usual. James Putnam spent his boyhood here, and later rose to be an eminent lawyer and the last Attorney General of the Province of Massachusetts under English rule. His friend John Adams called him "the best lawyer in America." A zealous loyalist, he took refuge in Boston in 1775 and ultimately accompanied the British army to England. Later he settled in St. John's, New Brunswick, as Judge of the Superior Court, but never returned to his native Danvers. The Putnam House was later owned by Timothy Pickering, the first Postmaster General, later Secretary of War and Secretary of State, who served under both Washington and John Adams. In later years John Greenleaf Whittier was a frequent visitor to the house. "Oak Knoll," his home for twenty years, is a few hundred yards away.

The Pardee-Morris House, in Morris Cove, New Haven, appears at first sight to be a contemporary country house of exceptional charm. Closer acquaintance will reveal it as one of the finest examples from the very early days of Connecticut, and a notable illustration of stone-end construction (Page 97). Its massive ends of masonry are still intact, despite a fire which was set by a marauding party of British in 1779. They contain eight stone fireplaces in all, two of them with Dutch ovens. There is a vaulted ballroom in the house, and, underneath, a huge kitchen with the oak beams exposed. The oyster shells used for lime in the mortar are still visible. In the coach house are two exceptionally fine old vehicles, a coach and a gig. Those who are attracted by the fragrance and color of old-time gardens will find an herb garden of unusual charm adjoining the house.

Visitors to Cape Cod will do well to stop at a sunny white structure in Yarmouthport, known in the neighborhood as "The 1680 House" (Page 98). Here again the original heart of the house is well obscured, and one is apt to pay more attention to the exhibits of silverware and old period pieces which furnish the rooms. Some fine old panelling is to be seen.

One of the most dramatic episodes of the 19th of April, 1775, centered about the Jason Russell House in Arlington, then known as Menatomy (Page 99). Between four and five in the afternoon the retreating Britishers surprised a body of Minute-Men who were lying in wait, and drove them toward this house, where a savage fight at close quarters ensued. Jason Russell, a proud 58-year old farmer and eleven others were killed in the skirmish. Eight other Americans reached the cellar, and with guns trained on the cellar door, threatened death to any Red Coat who dared to come down. Thus these eight escaped. The house was in the open fields at that time, but is now surrounded by modern buildings. It contains many souvenirs of those memorable days, including some silverware made by Paul Revere.

Another house which once stood in the meadows is the compact little homestead in Quincy where the second President of the United States was born (Page 99). It is the same simple farmhouse type, built around a massive central chimney, whose fireplace is nine feet wide and six feet deep. The floor boards are extremely wide and the inner walls are lined with brick. The house was owned by the Adams family until 1941, when it was given to the City of Quincy. A stone's throw away is an earlier house, almost identical in appearance, where John Adams' son, John Quincy Adams, was born (Page 82).

Every line in the Parson Capen House bespeaks its English ancestry (Pages 100-102). The town of Topsfield granted this land to the Reverend Joseph Capen in 1682. The Parson's bride, who came from the prominent Appleton family in Ipswich, wanted a new and larger parsonage, and this astonishing English manor house was the result. In England the house would doubtless have been finished in half timber instead of clapboards, but aside from this the similarity is perfect, and it is reasonable to believe that the house was built by skilled craftsmen who were fresh arrivals from the mother country. The second story has a wide structural overhang, ornamented by hewn drops. The gable ends of the attic also project, and are embellished with drops. It is a memorable experience to come upon this weathered veteran for the first time. The parson and his bride lie buried side by side on a hillside burial ground not far away.

In the grounds of the Essex Institute of Salem is the fine old gabled John Ward House, richly Elizabethan in character (Page 103). Its overhang is unusually wide, almost enough to give protection from the rain, as it did in England. Inside the house are several fascinating interiors. One contains an early Salem hearth with all the household implements of those days. Another is an Apothecary's Shop, complete with equipment, as it would have looked about 1830, and there is an unbelievable picturesque "Cent Shop" of the early 19th Century which will warm the heart of any antiquarian.

Few spots in New England are as well known as the Wayside Inn (Pages 104-107), in South Sudbury, Mass. The Inn's "Immigrant Ancestor" was John Howe who came to this country in 1638 and settled in Sudbury. His son Samuel, a carpenter by trade, built the present Inn building in 1686, and it remained open as an Inn until 1860, when Lyman Howe, the 5th generation of Howe landlords, died a bachelor. The original tavern sign, with names of the first three proprietors, is still preserved. Ezekiel Howe, third landlord in line, led 300 Sudbury men at North Bridge in Concord. George Washington stopped with Ezekiel in 1789, and Lafayette paid the Inn a visit during his memorable trip in 1824. The Inn was the first halt for the Western Mail Coach from Boston, and a favorite stopping place for farmers en route to market. Henry Wadsworth Longfellow came here in the 1840's and acquired the habit of spending part of his summers here.

When his "Tales of a Wayside Inn" was published, the Inn became known by that name. From 1860 to 1896 the house was not licensed as an inn, the only time in its long life that it ceased to operate as such. In 1923 Henry Ford purchased it, still maintaining it as an inn, and restoring many atmospheric touches, including an old-fashioned formal garden. The original tavern is of the central-hall type, with four large rooms and two fireplaces. One of these was the Tap Room with a high railed bar and a "portcullis" which could be lowered when the bar was closed. Four other rooms were named for famous visitors: Lafayette, Longfellow, Parsons and Edison. The parlor where Long-fellow pictured his friends telling "The Tales of a Wayside Inn" has the greatest literary interest. The celebrated ballroom where Lafayette danced is in a wing. On the top floor under the spacious gambrel roof are seven rooms still open to travelers. Meals are served regularly, and the cooking is in the best New England tradition. On the grounds are an old grist mill in operation and the "Martha-Mary Chapel," newest addition to this memorable estate which now comprises 3000 acres. Not only the Wayside Inn but the surrounding countryside has been restored to its appearance in the time of the Howe landlords.

The oldest house on Nantucket Island is a spare, shingled veteran with a low sweeping lean-to roof (Page 107). It was built in 1686 by Peter Coffin as a wedding present to his son, Jethro Coffin and his sixteen-year old bride. It is sometimes referred to as the "Horseshoe House," due to the peculiar horseshoe design outlined in brick on the chimney, a possible charm against witches. The house substantially retains its original form, even to the closet in an upstairs bedroom where an Indian once hid and frightened the day-lights out of the young housewife.

Around 1687 Eleazer Arnold built himself a stone-end house north of Providence, so far in the wilderness that it was referred to as "the end of the world" (Page 108). Its massive stone chimney, encasing a fireplace ten feet nine inches wide, is the best preserved in the state, and is crowned with pilasters as a final touch of distinction. Eleazer Arnold kept a fine tavern here, and reserved one old bed to accommodate Indians. The house is located in the township of Lincoln which, with its neighbor Smithfield, harbors some of the finest old house in New England.

One appreciates the background of the great poet of New England, John Greenleaf Whittier, after visiting his birthplace and the scene of his boy-hood (Page 109). A poetic farm it is, grown with magnificent trees, and bordered with willow-lined country roads. The homestead is definitely two rooms deep, but one massive brick chimney still suffices. The original frame of the house was built by an ancestor of the poet in 1688. Exhibited within are household articles owned by Whittier, many of them mentioned in "Snowbound."

One of New England's most idyllic villages is Old Deerfield, Mass., located in the fertile Connecticut Valley. A few of its old houses can be visited. Each of them bears a faint touch of tragedy, dating back to the horrible Deerfield Massacres. One of them is the Old Bloody Brook Tavern, built before 1700 in South Deerfield as a garrison house and tavern to protect travelers going North to Old Deerfield (Page 109). Later it was moved to the present site. Its walls are made of six inch hand hewn timbers. Its three massive fireplaces and old pine panels have been preserved, and the original writing on the walls is still visible.

The beautiful Frary House in Old Deerfield (Page 110), the only house to survive the Indian raids, (although its owner did not), offers numerous enticements to the visitor. One of them is the magnificent ballroom which was so popular when the house was run as a tavern by Selah Barnard. It has recently been restored and furnished in the style which flourished before the Revolution. The trustees of Deerfield Academy held their first meeting in this room in April 1797. Recently, on the 150th anniversary of this occasion, the present trustees of the Academy met in the same room. Samson Frary, one of the first settlers in this wilderness outpost, built the house, probably in the 1680's. Almost a century later it was serving as a tavern, and greatly in favor with the Tories of the village. During the Revolution the tavern's most notorious guest, Benedict Arnold, came here to buy fifteen thousand pounds of beef for his troops. During the 19th Century the house encountered varied vicissitudes until it was bought and saved from destruction by Miss C. Alice Baker.

More heroic rescue work was done on the Abraham Browne Jr. House in Watertown (Pages 111, 112) with the result that this unique house, built about 1690 and badly in need of repair, was saved and restored. Its two outstanding possessions are a tremendous fireplace, spanned by a hewn oak lintel, and the only original 3-part window frame known in New England. The house was enlarged in 1920.

Few houses are more closely associated with the *Mayflower* than the Old Brewster House in Kingston (Page 113). It has always remained in the Brewster family, and contains many relics which have been passed down from one generation to the other since the family landed in Plymouth in 1620. The house was built in 1690 by William Bradford, son of the pioneer Governor, for his step-son Joseph Holmes, who was about to embark upon the sea of matrimony with Miss Mary Brewster, grand-daughter of the Elder. Around 1720 Mary exchanged farms with her uncle, Wrestling Brewster, whose direct descendants occupied this house for the next two centuries. A wing was added during the Revolution when Thomas Brewster hung a sign outside the door, "Refreshment for Man & Beast," and served meals to travelers between Boston and the Cape. The house occupies a fine pine-covered spot on the original site given to Governor Bradford by the King.

The Glebe House in Woodbury (Page 114) enjoys both architectural and ecclesiastical distinction. It was the home of the Rev. John Rutgers Marshall. In a front room a Council meeting of ten Connecticut clergymen met on March 25, 1783 and selected Samuel Seabury to be sent to Aberdeen, Scotland, to be consecrated as the first Episcopal bishop in America. The house, which probably began with one room, has a rare combination of gambrel and lean-to roof. Inside is some fine panelling and a secret stairway. concealed behind a sliding panel. The Rev. Marshall, rector of St. Paul's, had occasional need to use this secret passage during the Revolutionary period.

Lexington, "the birthplace of American liberty," is rich in things architectural as well as historical. Three of the outstanding buildings associated with the fateful 19th of April, 1775, are open to the public, and all three date from the last decade of the 17th century. Two of them are taverns, and the other is the celebrated Hancock-Clarke House. The Buckman Tavern (Pages 114, 115), earliest of the three, remains substantially as it was the day when the Minute-Men, learning of the approach of the British, assembled here in the old tap room to await more definite word. From its windows, Paul Revere witnessed the arrival of the British, and later in the day two wounded Red Coats were brought inside for first aid, one of them dying shortly after. The scars of British bullets are still to be seen in its walls. John Buckman, a member of Captain Parker's company, was then landlord of the tavern, which was the oldest of Lexington's many inns. It was more aristocratic than the others, being for carriage folk rather than farmers.

There were many other contemporary taverns of interest built toward the end of the 17th century. One was the rural inn maintained by "Drummer" Samuel Stetson, in Hanover Center (Page 116). Another was the weathered old Parker Tavern in Reading (Page 116), where officers of the Scottish Highlanders were held captive during the Revolution. The tavern is well described by a nearby inscription: "The simple home of an ordinary man, not wealthy, not particularly distinguished, but a type of the God-fearing yeomanry . . . . as Ephriam Parker left it, it remains today, an unchanged relic in the midst of a changing world."

About a mile east of Lexington's Battle Green is another tavern, kept at the time by Sergeant William Munroe (Page 117). When Earl Percy arrived in Lexington he commandeered the tavern as his headquarters and hospital. Mrs. Munroe and her children hid in the woods near the house while the soldiers refreshed themselves at the tavern's expense. Sergeant Munroe received General Washington here years after the war, and served him dinner in the parlor. The chairs, table, dishes and hatrack used for that occasion are still preserved. The Munroe Tavern was said to be a favorite with turkey drovers, who would spend the night here while en route to the Boston market. On such occasions their herds of turkeys would roost in the surrounding trees with rather startling effect. One of the earlier Masonic Lodges in Massachusetts was formed in the Tavern in 1797, William Munroe being the first master.

Behind a curtain of century-old English beeches sits a house which recalls the dark period of the witchcraft trials. This is the venerable Hale House in Beverly (Page 118), built by the Reverend John Hale. Although a man of great learning and ability, John Hale joined in the Salem prosecutions until the charge of witchcraft was brought against his own wife. The lofty character of this gentle woman was so far about suspicion that this accusation against her broke the entire spell, and the witchcraft hysteria died away. Among John Hale's descendents were the martyred Nathan Hale, (whose fire brigade bucket is on exhibition within), and the noted Reverend Edward Everett Hale.

Few houses have the historical interest of the Hancock-Clarke House (Pages 118, 119). The original homestead was the little gambrel-roofed ell which the Rev. John Hancock built in 1698, and where five Hancock children were born and reared to manhood and womanhood. The main part of the house was added in 1734 by the second son, Thomas Hancock, who had become a prosperous Boston merchant. This made a house of eight rooms, with seven fireplaces and much fine woodwork. The third pastor of the village, Rev. Jonas Clarke, occupied the house upon taking up his duties in 1755, and became a trusted friend and advisor of John Hancock, the Governor and most conspicuous Signer of the Declaration of Independence. When events began to move fast in mid-April, John Hancock and his friend Samuel Adams found it natural to come to this house to remain with Parson Clarke, and they were sleeping here when Paul Revere aroused them in the early morning. Open country then surrounded the parsonage and the firing on the Common was plainly visible from these windows. The house is now a museum of extraordinary interest, which must be seen to be appreciated. All three of these Lexington houses, in fact, are filled with significant relics of the Revolution.

An accurate reproduction of the Indian House in Old Deerfield has been built and furnished with antiques and Indian relics of the period of the fateful massacre in 1704. The original house was demolished in 1848, but its tomahawk-dented front door may still be seen in Memorial Hall. The present structure contains a loom over 200 years old, and there are classes in weaving and spinning wool and flax, using this old equipment. The house is weathered a deep brown (Page 120). Visitors to Old Deerfield will notice that many of the old houses bear no trace of paint, and have been weathered a rich dark brown. This brings out the interesting fact that many 17th Century houses never had a coat of paint at all, and were supposed to weather to near-blackness.

Such is the sun-baked tone of the historic Winslow House, in Marshfield (Page 120), which was built during the last glimmer of the 17th Century by Isaac Winslow, grandson of Governor Edward Winslow, *Mayflower* Pilgrim. During the next four generations it played an important part in the community, and many early Governors and leading citizens of Plymouth Colony were dined there. The Winslows were ardent loyalists. During the Revolution the house was a stronghold for Tories. A company of British troops was once quartered within. Daniel Webster, who owned the adjoining estate, bought the house in 1830. It is a building of fine proportion, with a wide gabled roof, wooden quoins, pilastered chimney and a projecting entrance porch. Inside are many good fireplaces, one of which conceals a secret passage, some first rate panelling, and "Jacobean" front stairs.

The dawn of Civilization in New England is pictured in THE PIONEERS' VILLAGE, Salem, Mass., a careful reproduction of the windswept wilderness which was Salem in 1630.

55

In THE PIONEERS' VILLAGE, Salem, are reconstructed the earliest habitations of the Colonists, from bark-covered wigwams to the comparative opulence of the "Governor's fayre house."

"APTUCXET," Bourne, Mass., Plymouth Colony's first trading post, was established by Governor Bradford on this site in 1627. This permanent replica has been built upon its foundations.

THE FAIRBANKS HOUSE, Dedham, Mass., built in 1636 from oak timbers brought from England, is believed by some to be the oldest frame structure now standing in the United States.

To the FAIRBANKS HOUSE belongs another distinction, that of being one of the most picturesque of all our old houses. Its many roofs interlock in a fascinating manner.

Since Jonathan Fayerbanke built the house and occupied it with his wife and six children in 1636, 84 members of the Fairbanks family lived in it continuously up to 1903.

The facade of the HARTWELL FARM, Lincoln, Mass., is subtly unsymmetrical. It seems almost juvenile in comparison to the arboreal giant which stands sentry before it. The British marched past here on the way to Concord, April 19, 1775.

The ancient rooms of the HARTWELL FARM (1636-1639) have been stripped of thick coats of paint and wallpaper, revealing fine panelling and a noble kitchen fireplace. This is one of the two ground floor front rooms.

The DEANE WINTHROP HOUSE, Winthrop, Mass., is one of the earliest "salt box" houses. It was built in 1637 by Captain William Pierce, who piloted some of the first Puritans to Salem in 1629.

The BALCH HOUSE, Beverly, Mass. The small original house was built about 1638, and three additions were made before the house attained its present proportions.

JOHN BALCH was one of the earliest transatlantic travelers, landing in Weymouth
in 1623, later returning to England to be married. Back he came to Salem with his
bride, and years later built the oldest part of this Beverly house.

There are no frills evident in the frugal interior of the BALCH HOUSE. Spinning and weaving were done in this partly sheathed room, while the family meals were prepared at the small hearth.

The WALTER FYLER HOUSE, Windsor, Conn., built in 1640, stood inside palisades of high stakes when it was first built. Later its gambrel sheltered Windsor's first postoffice.

The HENRY WHITFIELD HOUSE, Guilford, Conn., built in 1639 by the Rev.
Henry Whitfield, founder of the town, is the oldest stone house in New England.
Recently it has been carefully restored.

A massive oak lintel was needed to support the masonry of the fireplace in the Great
Hall of the HENRY WHITFIELD HOUSE. It had two flues, permitting a fire in
one or both ends, as the weather demanded. The fireplace opening is 10 feet 4 inches
wide.

The WHIPPLE HOUSE, Ipswich, Mass., is very close to the English tradition. Its earliest construction dates from around 1638-40, and documents speak of several additions.

The husky, chamfered "summer" beams of this room in the WHIPPLE HOUSE
were long enough to cross and reinforce each other. The atmosphere of a cheerful
old English taproom pervades these pleasantly primitive surroundings.

The old HART HOUSE in Ipswich, Mass., bears the date of 1640 proudly on its
wide brick chimney. The period rooms of this house are so fine that some of them
have been reproduced or moved to the American Wing of the Metropolitan Museum
of Art.

The JOHN WARD HOUSE, Haverhill, Mass., was built some time before 1645 by the town's first minister. The earliest framed house in Haverhill, it is amazingly well preserved.

One can readily imagine the pioneer pastor sitting before his fire in the one-room JOHN WARD HOUSE while his good wife busied herself with the cooking. But there were also Indians and wolves to worry about, and a musket had to be handy over the hearth.

The OLD IRONWORKS HOUSE, Saugus, Mass. (original built before 1640), shows in its restored form the close relationship between the early New England houses and the rural English manors.

The commodious hearth of the OLD IRONWORKS HOUSE is fitted with a battery of ingenious implements from churns and candle moulds to toasters and trivets. It is a good place to dry herbs, too.

The old EMERSON-HOWARD HOUSE in Ipswich contains an excellent example of the narrow front hall and steep stairway clinging to the chimney stack, which occurs so often in 17 Century houses.

The EMERSON-HOWARD HOUSE, Ipswich, Mass., is said to have been built before 1648 by Thomas Emerson, ancestor of the philosopher. The house has a narrow hewn overhang, and infinite charm.

The DAGGETT HOUSE, Pawtucket, R. I., has seen many changes since its nucleus was built, supposedly around 1644. It is now set in idyllic surroundings in Slater Park.

Largely ignored by the public is the JAMES BLAKE HOUSE in Edward Everett Square, Boston. Originally built in 1648, it is a well restored example of a steep-roofed Elizabethan house.

The MACY-COLBY HOUSE, Amesbury, Mass., was built about 1650 by Thomas Macy, first Town Clerk of Amesbury. Macy later fled into exile in Nantucket when accused by a Puritan minister of harboring a Quaker.

The PAUL REVERE HOUSE, Boston, home of the great patriot from 1770 to 1800,
is the oldest building in the city. Built about 1650, it was restored to its original
condition in 1908.

The exterior of the TRISTRAM COFFIN HOUSE, Newbury, is weathered and vine grown. According to tradition, the centenary of Newbury was celebrated before this house in 1735.

The TRISTRAM COFFIN HOUSE, Newbury, Mass., began with a small building (now an ell), built about 1651. This fine old fireplace, framed in panelling, is somewhat later.

One of the few "butteries" still preserved intact is in the TRISTRAM COFFIN HOUSE, Newbury, complete with churns, milk stools, wooden bowls and even a milkmaid's yoke.

The pewter-lined cupboards of the TRISTRAM COFFIN HOUSE reveal the in-
genuity of the early cabinet makers. Joshua Coffin, historian of Newbury, lived in
this house.

The OLD ORDINARY, Hingham, Mass. (built 1650), is a splendid example of the
early wayside inn. The tap room and many other hospitable features are still
preserved.

The "SCOTCH"-BOARDMAN HOUSE, Saugus, Mass., was built in 1651 to house Scotch prisoners who were captured in the Battle of Dunbar and brought to Saugus to work in the old ironworks.

The "SCOTCH"-BOARDMAN HOUSE, Saugus, is one of the best preserved 17th century houses in New England, and its date of 1651 one of the earliest to be authenticated by documents.

The JOHN ALDEN HOUSE, Duxbury, Mass., was built in 1653 by Jonathan Alden, third son of John and Priscilla, who later lived in it. The house has never been owned outside the Alden family.

The OLD GAOL, York Village, Maine, is claimed to be the oldest public building in the United States. Its dungeons are still intact. Now a summer museum.

The KENDALL HOLMES HOUSE, Plymouth, Mass. (built circa 1653) was the first homestead of William Harlow, who later built another famous gambrel-roofed house from the timbers of the Old Fort. The sturdy framework of the house, its fine stairway and its great central chimney are still intact.

The COOPER-FROST-AUSTIN HOUSE, Cambridge, Mass., built about 1657 by
John Cooper, Deacon of the First Church in Cambridge, is the oldest house in the city,
and one of the finest.

The COOPER-FROST-AUSTIN HOUSE, Cambridge, possesses several notable
fireplaces built around its chimney stack, which terminates with a fine pilastered top.

The CORNET JOSEPH PARSONS HOUSE, oldest in Northampton, Mass., was built in 1658 by the city's pioneer settler and founder of the Parsons family in America.

The JAMES BABSON COOPERAGE SHOP, Gloucester, Mass., was built in 1659 by James Babson, barrel-maker, who came to America in 1632. It is one of New England's first stone buildings.

The HYLAND HOUSE, Guilford, Conn., dating from about 1660 and rebuilt in 1720, has a subtle hewn overhang. In this house Ebenezer Parmelee built the first town clock in America.

The WITCH HOUSE in Salem, Mass. is markedly Elizabethan in character. Built before 1662, it was the home of Jonathan Corwin, one of the judges at the witch-craft trials.

The CLAFLIN-RICHARDS HOUSE, Wenham, Mass., was built in 1663-64 by Robert Macklafflin, presumably one of the Scotch prisoners captured by Cromwell in the Battle of Dunbar in 1650.

The THOMAS LEE HOUSE, East Lyme, Conn., dating from about 1660, began as a single room with chamber above, but expanded to make room for the owner's fifteen children.

The STANLEY-WHITMAN HOUSE, Farmington, Conn., built about 1660, is an unusual "salt-box," with a great central stone chimney and a wide framed overhang embellished by four hewn "drops."

The JOHN QUINCY ADAMS BIRTHPLACE, Quincy, Mass., (built 1663), was the home of John and Abigail Adams during the Revolution. At that time it was surrounded by open fields, which since have been transformed into city streets.

The RICHARD JACKSON HOUSE, Portsmouth, N. H., built about 1664, is probably the oldest house in Portsmouth, and certainly the most picturesque. Two wings and an extremely long lean-to have been added to the original house.

The interiors of the RICHARD JACKSON HOUSE have a primitive simplicity which is appealing rather than austere. Much of its ancient wide panelling is still intact.

The JABEZ HOWLAND HOUSE, Plymouth, Mass. is the oldest house in this historic town, dating from 1666. It was purchased, repaired and furnished by the descendants of John Howland in 1913.

The STEPHEN DANIELS HOUSE in Salem, Mass. dates from 1667. Two immense fireplaces are imbedded in its central chimney. The house contains a remarkable collection of antiques.

The HOUSE OF SEVEN GABLES, Salem, Mass. (built 1668), has, of course, been
immortalized by Hawthorne's romance of the same name. Architecturally it has almost
as much of interest.

The HOUSE OF SEVEN GABLES, Salem, was formerly known as the Turner-Ingersoll House. Hawthorne came here frequently to see his spinster cousin, Susan Ingersoll, and was one of the few men permitted to cross the threshold.

The great chamber on the second floor of the HOUSE OF SEVEN GABLES was "Phoebe's Room" in Hawthorne's classic. Among other pieces, it contains a Queen Anne highboy and a fine Salem chest.

The HATHAWAY HOUSE, Salem, Mass. (built 1682), formerly called "The Old Bakery," was rescued when about to be turned over to the house wreckers, and moved to join the House of Seven Gables group.

The kitchen-living room of the HATHAWAY HOUSE gives a vivid picture of the early pioneer's hearthside, though few pioneers probably had as fine a collection of pewter and crockery as is now on display.

The RETIRE BECKETT HOUSE is the oldest of the House of Seven Gables group in Salem, dating from 1655. This wintry view gives scant hint of the charm of this spot in summer, when luncheon and tea are served under the arbor.

The EELS-STOWE HOUSE, Milford, Conn. (built 1669) was used as a hospital during the Revolution. Captain Stephen Stowe and his wife, Freelove Baldwin, lived here.

The SWETT-ILSLEY HOUSE, Newbury, Mass. (in the distance), was built before 1670. The first newspaper in Newbury was printed here. Later it was a chocolate works and also a tavern.

The SWETT-ILSLEY HOUSE, Newbury, began as a one-room house of two floors and grew by segments. This fireplace is small compared to that which flourished in the old tap room, this being over ten feet wide.

The CHAPLIN-CLARKE-WILLIAMS HOUSE, Rowley, Mass. (built about 1671), is a picturesque farmhouse, embedded in the hillside. It has a lean-to roof and two hewn overhangs at one end.

The MAJOR JOHN BRADFORD HOUSE, Kingston, Mass. (built 1674). To this house the grandson of Governor Bradford brought his bride, Mercy Warren, also grandchild of a Mayflower Pilgrim.

The venerable kitchen of the MAJOR JOHN BRADFORD HOUSE is warm and inviting, a very satisfactory spot for the evening meal on a cold winter's night. The furniture and utensils, together with an ancient loom, are all of the period.

The WANTON-LYMAN-HAZARD HOUSE, Newport, R. I. (built about 1675) effectively re-creates the atmosphere of Newport in its early days. Many notable antiques grace its old rooms.

The HARLOW HOUSE, Plymouth, Mass., was built in 1677 from timbers of the old Pilgrim Fort on Burial Hill, and is a splendidly preserved example of the homes of the first Mayflower descendants.

A fine old hand loom still functions in the low studded kitchen of the HARLOW HOUSE. During the summer, demonstrations are given here of early household industries—weaving, spinning, dyeing, cooking and candle making.

The PLATTS-BRADSTREET HOUSE, Rowley, Mass. (built about 1677) stands on land that was granted to William Bellingham before 1643. Adjoining it is a unique one-room shoe shop.

The kitchen-dining room of the PLATTS-BRADSTREET HOUSE is notable for its beautiful feathered sheathing and for the fittings of its hospitable hearth.

The REBECCA NURSE HOUSE, Danvers, Mass., was built in 1678 by Francis Nurse, whose wife Rebecca was taken from this house and hanged as a witch in 1692, during the Salem witchcraft delusion. The favorite chair of the martyred woman, mother of nine children, is on exhibit within.

This low room in the "lean-to" of the REBECCA NURSE HOUSE, Danvers, is partitioned with the typical wall surface of wide vertical planks molded at the edges, which graced many early Colonial houses.

The REBECCA NURSE HOUSE, Danvers, contains exceptionally fine examples of early low-ceilinged rooms. The loom and the spinning wheel were vital parts of the household.

The PETER TUFTS HOUSE, Medford, Mass., built about 1678 as a garrison house, is said to be the oldest brick building now standing in New England. Medford was celebrated for its early brick kilns.

The JAMES PUTNAM HOUSE, Danvers, Mass. (built 1680, 1715), was the birthplace of James Putnam, the great lawyer and staunch loyalist who accompanied the British Army back to England and never returned to his native land.

The PARDEE-MORRIS HOUSE, New Haven, Conn. (built about 1680-85), was burned, except for its stone ends and lintels, by the British, July 5, 1779. It was rebuilt the same year.

Natural pine panelling and a good bolection moulding surround this fireplace, one of eight built in the massive stone ends of the PARDEE-MORRIS HOUSE.

The nucleus of the COLONEL JOHN THACHER HOUSE, Yarmouthport, Mass., was built in 1680. The panelled rooms, which make an admirable setting for the display of old silver, are later.

The COLONEL JOHN THACHER HOUSE, in Yarmouthport, has several interiors which preserve the atmosphere of a prosperous Cape Cod home of the 18th century.

The JASON RUSSELL HOUSE, Arlington, Mass. (built about 1680), was in the thick of the fray on April 19, 1775. It still contains bullet holes made by the British in a skirmish around the house, in which Jason Russell and eleven Minute Men were killed.

The BIRTHPLACE OF PRESIDENT JOHN ADAMS, Quincy, Mass., dates from about 1660, and is the early homestead of the Adams family. There is a secret hiding place behind the panels of the fireplace.

The PARSON CAPEN HOUSE, Topsfield, Mass. (built 1683), is one of the most flawless examples of English manor house in America. Its setting and interiors are superb.

The **PARSON CAPEN HOUSE** bespeaks English precedent in almost every detail.
It is a framed overhang type, ornamented with hewn "drops." The leaded windows
are careful restorations.

The lower floor of the PARSON CAPEN HOUSE is furnished in the manner of the 17th century. The fireplaces, stair railing and newel, and many other parts are the originals.

The low living room of the PARSON CAPEN HOUSE is furnished with pieces of the same period, among them a gate-leg table and some slat-back Carver armchairs.

The JOHN WARD HOUSE, Salem, Mass. (built 1684), with steep gables and a substantial overhang, is rich in old English atmosphere. In the foreground is a cupola rescued from a Salem mansion.

The hearth of the JOHN WARD HOUSE, Salem, complete with kettles, brick ovens, mechanical spit and benches for the old and young, gives a revealing insight into the home life of the early colonists.

The WAYSIDE INN, South Sudbury, Mass., was built as a place of public entertainment in 1686 by Samuel Howe, and was run as an inn by his descendants until 1860. Known first as Howe's Tavern, then the "Red Horse Tavern," it became identified as the Wayside Inn after the publication of Longfellow's "Tales of a Wayside Inn" in 1863.

The Coach House of the WAYSIDE INN, South Sudbury, was built of old timbers in 1909. It houses two old stage coaches, one of which carried Lafayette to the laying of the cornerstone of Bunker Hill Monument in 1824.

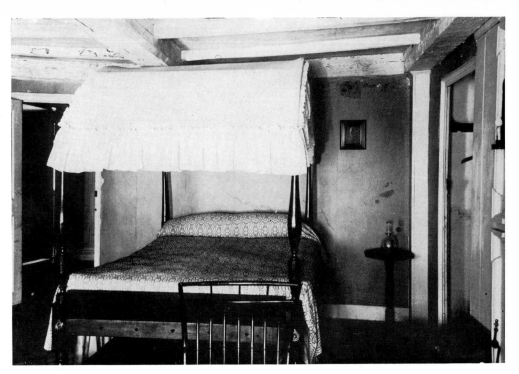

Many rooms of the WAYSIDE INN have been restored to their original 17th Century aspect. Some of the authentic Howe furnishings have been traced and brought back. The Wayside Inn is still maintained as a hostelry.

The ballroom of the WAYSIDE INN, with its orchestra platform, wide board floor and wooden seats built along the wall, is one of the Inn's most delightful features.

Many a convivial group has gathered about the table in this old panelled room of the WAYSIDE INN during the last two centuries, as they have in the old fashioned tap room farther front.

The REDSTONE SCHOOL HOUSE was brought to the WAYSIDE INN estate in 1927. This is the school referred to in "Mary had a little lamb," and sixteen youngsters from grades 1 to 4 are in daily attendance.

This old barn has been preserved in a sympathetic setting in the WAYSIDE INN grounds, and shelters some old stage coaches. An old fashioned grist mill has also been put in commission.

The oldest house on Nantucket Island is the JETHRO COFFIN HOUSE, built in 1686 by Peter Coffin as a wedding present to his son Jethro and his sixteen-year old bride.

The ELEAZER ARNOLD HOUSE, Lincoln, R. I. (built about 1687) is a stone-end house with an interesting wood facade. Its great stone fireplace, ten feet nine inches wide, is the largest in the state.

The gargantuan fireplace of the ELEAZER ARNOLD HOUSE is spanned by a fine oak lintel. The stone-end type is a rarity in New England, and this is perhaps the finest example extant.

The JOHN GREENLEAF WHITTIER HOMESTEAD, Haverhill, Mass. (built about 1688), is the birthplace of the beloved New England poet. A poet might well grow out of such surroundings.

The OLD BLOODY BROOK TAVERN in Old Deerfield, Mass. (built before 1700) was once a garrison and tavern, designed to give food, drink and lodging to the traveler along the Connecticut Valley, and to protect him from the Indians.

The only complete survivor of the 17th Century Indian raids on Old Deerfield is the lovely FRARY HOUSE, built in this frontier outpost about 1685 by the second settler, Samson Frary. He was murdered in the first Indian massacre.

In the 18th Century the FRARY HOUSE was converted into a tavern and was the favorite gathering place for the outstanding Tories of the village. Its beautiful ball-room has recently been restored.

The ABRAHAM BROWNE, JR. HOUSE, Watertown, Mass., built about 1690, is distinguished by an enormous fireplace, spanned by one massive lintel of oak. Much of the original framing has been exposed.

Rooms in the south portion of the ABRAHAM BROWNE, JR. HOUSE are lighted with three-part casement window frames, modeled after an original which was found in this house, and believed to be a unique survivor of its kind in New England.

The ABRAHAM BROWNE, JR. HOUSE, Watertown, contains several other fireplaces, one on a more imposing scale, and many of the simple furnishings of a 17th Century household.

The OLD BREWSTER HOUSE, Kingston, Mass., was built in 1690 by Governor Bradford's son William, who married Wrestling Brewster's daughter Mary. The sixth generation of Brewsters now live on the property.

The GLEBE HOUSE, Woodbury, Conn. (built 1690, 1740), is known as the Birthplace of American Episcopacy. It was the scene of the election of Bishop Samuel Seabury, first Episcopal bishop in the United States.

The BUCKMAN TAVERN, Lexington, Mass. (built 1690), facing the Battlegreen, is famed as the headquarters of the Minute-Men on that fateful day in April 1775.

Here in the Tap Room of the BUCKMAN TAVERN, Lexington, the Minute-Men assembled on the morning of April 19, 1775, to await definite word of the approach of the British troops.

The BUCKMAN TAVERN, Lexington, at present contains a noteworthy collection of Revolutionary relics. The first village store and the town's first postoffice were also located here.

The SAMUEL STETSON HOUSE, Hanover Center, Mass., was originally a one-room house, built about 1694. It was enlarged to its present size by "Drummer" Samuel Stetson in 1716.

The PARKER TAVERN, Reading, Mass. (built 1694), a fine old "salt-box," was used to house Colonel Archibald Campbell and other officers of the Scottish Highlanders after their capture in Boston Harbor, April 19, 1775.

The MUNROE TAVERN, Lexington, Mass. (built 1695), was used as headquarters and hospital for his wounded soldiers by Earl Percy, on April 19, 1775. George Washington dined here in 1789.

The bar room of the MUNROE TAVERN contains William Munroe's original tavern sign, cut out of a single piece of hard white pine, and many relics of his congenial reign as a landlord.

The HALE HOUSE in Beverly, Mass. was built in 1697 by the Reverend John Hale, ancestor of Nathan Hale and the Reverend Edward Everett Hale.

The HANCOCK-CLARKE HOUSE, Lexington, Mass. (built 1698). Here Samuel Adams and John Hancock were sleeping when aroused by Paul Revere on the night of April 19, 1775.

In the HANCOCK-CLARKE HOUSE, Lexington, John Hancock spent seven years of his boyhood. The house now contains an invaluable collection of relics from the Revolutionary War.

The INDIAN HOUSE MEMORIAL, Deerfield, Mass., is an accurate reproduction of the house built by Ensign John Sheldon in 1698, where captives were held during the Deerfield Massacre of 1704.

The historic WINSLOW HOUSE, Marshfield, Mass., was built in 1699 on the site of the estate of Governor Edward Winslow, Mayflower pilgrim, by one of his descendants. Daniel Webster owned the house for a time.

Open House in New England

Short House, Old Newbury, Mass.

IV

Eighteenth Century Houses

Architectural styles showed few perceptible changes with the turn of the century, but there were conclusive signs pointing to the demise of the central chimney cottage and the upsurge of the two-story, central hall type of dwelling, now referred to as "Colonial." The old Goulding House in South Sudbury (Page 141) shows no such tendency, however. In its present carefully restored form it belongs in the 17th Century, even though it was built a trifle later. It rejoices in a large stone fireplace, a large collection of early ironwork and some fine panelling.

In 1703, Phineas Upham was married to Miss Tamzen Hill in Malden, Mass., the Reverend Mr. Wigglesworth officiating. According to tradition, Phineas came to his new house in Melrose, "on horseback, with his bride, Tamzen riding behind him on a pillion." This is the evidence upon which the date of 1703 has been assigned to the sun-blackened old house on Page 141. The son and grandson of Phineas were both named Amos, and both lived in the house, as did Asa, son of the second Amos, who died there in 1869. By 1913 it was in a sorry condition, rapidly falling into decay, but was rescued and extensively restored. Now the hearthside where sat Phineas and Tamzen and their son Amos looks quite as it did two centuries ago.

The more the early builders employed the gambrel roof, the more flexible it became. Thus in the Fisher-Richardson House in Mansfield (Page 142) , the gambrel bridges an unusually wide span, producing a silhouette which clings nicely to the ground. The house contains some excellent interiors, good period furniture and an exhibition of early local industries. This was the home of the first miller of Mansfield and is located near the Taunton bounds, first surveyed by Miles Standish in 1640.

With the Dorothy Quincy Homestead in Quincy (Page 142) the Colonial mansion has definitely arrived. The house is almost square, covered with a hip roof and embellished with formal dormers and a top railing. Obviously a patrician estate, it is an early reflection of the prosperity that was coming to the Colonies. This was the birthplace of the high spirited young lady who became the wife of John Hancock. There is a secret chamber in the house where many a Colonial trooper reputedly found a hiding place.

Stephen Hopkins, ten times Governor of Rhode Island and Signer of the Declaration of Independence, has been called Providence's most distinguished citizen. The house which he built and in which he lived for over forty years has been moved to a hillside site and preserved for posterity (Page 143) . George Washington was his guest here, and the room where he slept is still shown, completely furnished.

Benjamin Thompson was an extraordinary man, a scientist and inventor, who cured smoky chimneys, invented cook stoves, cleared Munich of beggars and discovered "Heat as a Mode of Motion." While living in Bavaria he was created a Count of the Holy Roman Empire by Munich's Elector Maxmilian, and took the title of Count Rumford, from the old name of Concord, N. H., where he had lived for a time. His birthplace is a fine old house on the outskirts of Woburn, Mass. (Page 144) , within whose walls can be seen an original "Rumford Roaster." A charming English garden surrounds the house.

The only house which Nathaniel Hawthorne ever owned is "The Wayside," in Concord (Page 144) which he bought from the Alcotts and owned until his death in 1864. Here he built his famous tower study, a refuge from visitors added in 1860, and here are about a dozen pieces of his furniture still to be seen. Louisa May Alcott spent four years of her girlhood here, and described them later in "Little Women." The house was subsequently the home of "Margaret Sidney," and it was here that she wrote many volumes of "The Five Little Peppers." The Wayside richly deserves the title of "Home of Four Authors." On the 19th of April 1775 General Gage ordered his officers to search this house with particular care, since spies had reported that ammunition was concealed in a shop near the house. The interior of the house has been preserved much as it was when Emerson and Thoreau enjoyed its hospitality. Nineteenth Century additions do much to disguise the antiquity of the house, the central portion of which was built before 1717.

A patriarch of Cape Ann is the "Old Castle" in Pigeon Cove, a conventional central-chimney house, with a lean-to, hewn overhang and low ceilings (Page 145). Its timbers are suspected of being less conventional, however, for many of them appear to have been salvaged from wrecks along the neighboring shore. It is thought that the house was built for lumbermen who logged the town lands. It has been known as "The Old Castle" from the earliest time. It loomed up conspicuously on the shore, and may have looked to the old countrymen much like the castles on their own English coast. This is one explanation of its name.

An interesting group of historic buildings has been assembled on the slope of Prospect Hill in Harvard, Mass., a location which enjoys an overwhelming view of the broad valley beneath. One of the group is a peaceful old red house known as "Fruitlands," where Bronson Alcott and his friends attempted to realize a "New Eden" in 1843 (Page 146). Another is the Shaker Museum (Page 146), the oldest house built by the Shakers in the original Harvard Shaker village. The end chimneys in this frame house are a departure from tradition. Finally there is "The American Indian Museum," which contains a notable collection of prehistoric implements, and specimens of Indian art and industries.

A superb early mansion is the Warner House in Portsmouth (Page 147), probably the most elaborate in New England in its time. Portsmouth was a town of considerable affluence in the early 18th Century, and many of its citizens were men of wealth who were impressed with the more imposing three-story type of estate which flourished in England at that time. When Captain Archibald McPhaedris, "an immigrant from Scotland who made a fortune and married above his station," undertook to build this early Georgian mansion, he spent five years and over six thousand pounds to complete it. The house is a massive affair, with many fireplaces built into the substantial brick ends. On the walls of the staircase are some extraordinary primitive frescoes, dating from 1760, which have survived practically unblemished, due to the protection of several layers of wall paper. More soothing to the eyes are five portraits of members of the Warner family, painted by Blackburn in 1761. The rich carving of the woodwork adds immense style to the interiors, and it is not surprising that all distinguished visitors to the town were entertained here as a matter of course. Perched above the third-story dormers is a "captain's walk" and cupola overlooking Portsmouth harbor.

The Ropes Mansion in Salem (Pages 148, 149), affords an exceptionally accurate picture of the home of a wealthy Salem family, exactly as it looked during the city's great shipping days. The same family occupied the house from mid-18th century until 1907 when it was left by the wills of the Misses Ropes, together with a large garden and an endowment for Botanical studies, these three being known as the "Ropes Memorial." With the house were left all of the contents that had accumulated during a century and a half. Furniture and heirlooms and all the details of family life have thus been preserved in splendid condition. Of particular interest is a room devoted to the double set of Canton china and the rare table glass imported in 1816 for the wedding of Sally Ropes. The house is of the central-hall type with two side chimneys and a sizable wing behind. It was moved back from the street in 1894 and a formal garden has been achieved in the rear. A good deal of dignity has been lent by the imposing fence, with posts carved from a design by McIntire.

A rambling white mansion in Exeter, N. H., has claimed a succession of distinguished owners since Eliphalet Coffin first sold its plot of land to Nathaniel Ladd in 1721. The Ladd family owned it for 26 years, and then a noteworthy string of Gilmans took possession. In this family were many famous sons and grandsons, soldiers, financiers, Governors, Congressmen, U. S. Senators and Signers of the Constitution. At present it is the headquarters of the Society of the Cincinnati in the State of New Hampshire (Page 150). The interiors afford a splendid example of the fine panelling and woodwork which were executed in this period of good taste and careful workmanship.

Early Connecticut houses are often distinguished by wide overhanging gables, covered with large hand-hewn shingles which have been painted white. The Judson house in Stratford is a good example (Pages 150, 151). Within are several rooms of different periods, all of considerable interest. There is an ancient rustic fireplace, another one with panelling of later date, and some highly intriguing corner cupboards.

A Cape Cod cottage of the best sort is the Cudworth House (Page 151), even though it is situated in Scituate (the alliteration is too tempting to resist), many miles north of the Cape Cod canal.

Several generations of Harvard presidents occupied the old Wadsworth House in Cambridge, whose smiling white and yellow facade brightens up a corner of the Harvard Yard (Page 152). General Washington used the house as headquarters in 1775, but it proved too small, and he moved to the Vassall House. The corner clapboards of the Wadsworth house meet without the aid of corner boards, which means good carpentry. Originally there was a charming garden in front of the house, in the area which now rumbles with heavy traffic. The brick portion in the rear of this house was added in the 19th Century to serve as the President's office. At present the house is used by Harvard University, largely for alumni affairs.

The shingles of the old Martin House in Swansea (Page 153) are weather-beaten a silvery gray, very much as they are on Cape Cod. The tone contrasts with the sparkling white of the window trim, and produces an effect which is a joy to the eye. All that is needed are some rambler roses, and the Martin House has these too. Inside the visitor will find a good collection of old pewter, china, silverware and clocks.

In the beautiful farm lands near Newport is a sedate old house, embellished by a wide, well carved doorway and sheltered by enormous trees. It seems too patrician to be a mere farmhouse. Closer inspection, in fact, will reveal it to be "Whitehall," the country home of Dean Berkeley, the philosopher and poet, later Lord Bishop of Cloyne, Ireland. Here he penned many of his philosophical works. Later it was run as a "Public House" by Gilbert Stuart's grandfather. British officers and men were quartered here during the Revolution. The wide doorway and windows show fine carpentry (Page 153).

South Egremont, in the Berkshires, is another of those flawless New England villages which delight the traveler and artist alike. The town has several hospitable shrines, including an inn, a weaving shop, a blacksmith's shop and a tavern (Page 154), which has retained the atmosphere of the stagecoach days. Sir William Johnson, the special envoy of George III stopped here regularly on his trips along the old turnpike between Albany and Hartford. The old Egremont Tavern still provides a comfortable, epicurean and quite memorable stopping place for the traveler.

One of New England's most distinguished estates, particularly from the point of view of its history and ownership, is the Adams Mansion in Quincy (Page 154). Built by Major Leonard Vassall of Boston in 1731, it was purchased by John Adams in 1787 and occupied by the Adams family for the next 140 years, during which time many additions were made. Both Adams Presidents lived in the house, as did Charles Francis Adams, Minister to England. The house is now an Adams Family Memorial, furnished and maintained, with the formal garden, exactly as if the family were there. An impressive collection of family portraits, among them some of the finest works of Copley and Gilbert Stuart, Abigail Adams' bedroom with the family cradle, the desk of John Adams and the chair in which he died, the library and the household furniture, all of these are to be seen.

According to tradition, General Israel Putnam was shaving in his room in Knapp's Tavern, Greenwich, Conn., on the morning of February 26, 1779, when he perceived the gleam of a Red Coat in his mirror. The General lost no time in securing his safety by jumping on his horse and plunging at a full trot down a nearby precipice where his pursuers dared not follow. A bullet went through the General's hat, but he was uninjured and continued on to Stamford. There he gathered reinforcements and returned to Greenwich, where he captured fifty Britishers and two wagon loads of plunder which they were about to take away. Knapp's Tavern has been preserved, and is now Putnam Cottage (Page 155), as charming a bit of old architecture as will be found along the Post Road today.

The Royall House in Medford (Pages 155, 156) is hard to classify, since it apparently dates from four different periods, the oldest of which may go back to a very ancient farmhouse built by Governor Winthrop. What the eye sees now is an imposing mansion with brick ends, built in 1732. Fine carpentry is evident in the window casements, and inside are some of the best examples of wood carving of the period. It was distinctly a patrician estate. On the premises was a brick building used as slave quarters, one of the very few of its kind in Massachusetts. The mansion was used as Headquarters for Stark's Division during the Siege of Boston. Generals Washington, Stark, Lee and Sullivan met here and planned the siege. Among the exhibits is one of the original tea chests recovered from the Boston Tea Party.

An unforgettable stretch of New England road begins at High Street in Newburyport and leads southward toward Rowley. For miles on either side of this broad, sheltered highway, will be found a succession of splendid old houses, some of them farms, some of them quite imposing estates. One of the finest is the Short House (Page 157) whose ends are built of beautifully weathered brick. The interior woodwork in two of the rooms is extremely fine. The paint has been removed from the panelling, exposing the skillful carving in the full length pilasters which flanked many mantels of the period. The use of a simple bolection moulding was all that the fireplaces required. The china cupboard, placed with a refreshing lack of symmetry, adds much to the charm of the formal parlor.

Another completely furnished picture of the 18th Century can be found in the Mission House in Stockbridge (Page 158). Nothing in the rooms of this historic structure is older than 1749, and some of the furniture belonged to John Sergeant, for whom the house was built. In 1734 Sergeant was appointed the first missionary to the Housatonic Indians, at the request of the Indians themselves. He gave up his position as tutor in Yale College and was ordained in Deerfield before a distinguished audience, including the Governor, the Council and many Indians. His salary: 100 pounds a year. The most noteworthy architectural feature of the house is its elaborate doorway, conceived in the best Connecticut Valley tradition.

In the busy heart of Cambridge (Page 159) is the gambrel-roofed house long occupied by William Brattle, successively physician, preacher and lawyer. He did well in his last chosen profession, becoming Attorney General in 1736. Brattle was also a Brigadier General of His Majesty's Provincial troops, and such a staunch Royalist that he fled with the British to Halifax after the evacuation of Boston. Small wonder that Brattle Street became known as "Tory Row." The house is now the headquarters of the Cambridge Social Union.

The Nathaniel Allis House in Madison (Page 159) is best known as the home of Cornelius Bushnell, who helped to finance the building of the *Monitor* at the time of the Civil War. The interior of this house has been preserved, not as a museum but as an old dwelling of the period, with each room furnished with minute care.

Few houses now standing in New England are as closely associated with George Washington and his wife as the Tobias Lear House, in Portsmouth (Page 160). Tobias Lear, after graduating from Harvard in 1783, became Private Secretary to George Washington, residing almost continually with the Washington family during a period of fourteen years, during which time he enjoyed the complete confidence of the first President. Twice a widower, he successively married nieces of Martha Washington, and was frequently sent on diplomatic missions abroad. The house, built by Lear's grandfather about 1740, is interesting as an early square type with a distinctive hipped roof and a good, simple doorway and panelling.

Another man who enjoyed Washington's confidence was Oliver Ellsworth, one of Connecticut's great legal minds. He was one of the committee of five that drafted the Constitution, later a Senator to the First Congress and after that was appointed third Chief Justice of the United States by Washington in 1796. Under President Adams he was Envoy Extraordinary and Minister Plenipotentiary to France. Both Presidents visited the imposing old Ellsworth homestead in Windsor (Page 160). Its agreeable two-story porch treatment, in which the columns are stretched considerably in their wooden version, was added to the house by Oliver Ellsworth, making it resemble some of the old Litchfield houses. The older part, built in 1740 by David Ellsworth, the stateman's father, is one of the earliest of the central hall type. Inside are exhibited many of the possessions gathered by the envoy in his travels, including a square of Gobelins tapestry presented to him by Napoleon Bonaparte.

The attractive little Edward Devotion House, in the heart of Brookline, is, in its present form, a departure from the conventional, since its central doorway is off-center. The house seems to be waiting wistfully for another wing to be added, to achieve its missing symmetry. This house (Page 161) was on the route followed by William Dawes when he rode to meet Paul Revere on April 19, 1775. When his historic ride is re-enacted on each April 18th, "William Dawes" and his escort always stop at the house.

A simple old white house in Bernardston, Mass., near Greenfield, contains quite a curiosity, a bit of mural decoration supposedly painted by a British spy during the War of 1812 (Page 161). A mysterious stranger came to the town about that time, and did the mural work to pay for his board and lodging. His painting kept him busy for months, but one day some equally mysterious men arrived from New York State and carried him away. The supposition has always been that he was arrested as a spy. The paintings are still fresh and colorful. The house also contains much old furniture.

Robert Hooper, merchant prince and philanthropist, was known as "King" Hooper, not so much for his regal scale of living as for his fairness and integrity in dealing with his sailors. He gave the town of Marblehead its first fire engine, its first wharf and, as the town's leading citizen, established an academy of learning there. In 1745, at the age of thirty-eight, King Hooper moved his father's house back, turned it at right angles to the street, and then built a graceful three-story house in front of it (Pages 162, 163). The result is one of the most interesting, if not most coherent house in New England. Hooper was married four times, once to the daughter of General Glover, and had eleven children. After his death in 1790 the house was used by a son, John Hooper. Later Jason Chamberlain traded his schooner *Economy* for it. In more recent years it was adapted as a drygoods shop, as the local Y.M.C.A. and finally as a summer antique shop. At a moment when it risked being converted into tenements the mansion was acquired by the Marblehead Arts Association, under whose direction it has been largely restored. The graceful banquet hall, lighted by delicate chandeliers and heated by two fireplaces, where Hooper once entertained lavishly, now serves as an art gallery. The cabin room, the cellar kitchen and the wine room have been restored, and an 18th Century garden stretches behind the lofty rear gambrel. Much of the original stencil work is still visible.

A Connecticut parsonage of interest is the old Mansfield House in Ansonia (Page 163) whose overhanging gable and 24-pane windows are worthy of note. The Reverend Richard Mansfield, for whom the house was built, served as rector of St. James' Episcopal parish for 72 years, apparently a record, and died at the age of 96. The house originally stood under the shade of spreading trees, commanding a view of the Naugatuck Valley from an old Indian trail. It was moved to its present location in 1925.

It was in the tap room of the Wright Tavern in Concord (Page 164), that British officers boasted they would "stir the Yankee blood before night." This old inn remains little changed since that 19th of April, 1775, when it served as British headquarters. The old tap room is still intact, and with it the original semi-circular bar and a drop-leaf tavern table long the property of Paul Revere's family. An original British red coat is one of the most appropriate exhibits. The cellar of the tavern was originally used as the village bakery, and its picturesque fireplace with large brick oven is still in place. The building has one of the early square hipped roofs and faces the Meeting House Green. Good New England meals add to the charm of this notable old tavern, and assure the visitor of the gastronomic success of his Concord trip. The Wright Tavern is under the same management as the nearby Country Store, a rather unique "open house" in itself.

In a large, gambrel-roofed homestead far out in the Rhode Island countryside Gilbert Stuart first saw the light of day (Page 164). In the basement is the little mill where Gilbert Stuart's father ground snuff for a living. Adjoining this is the grist mill where early Rhode Islanders ground their corn. From such humble surroundings the young artist rose to be a worthy painter; then went to England to study with Benjamin West and Sir Joshua Reynolds, and returned after the Revolution, an acknowledged master. His was an enviable and cosmopolitan existence, always distinguished by his charm, good humor and gift of repartee. But at the end of his career, which included close to 700 portrait commissions, he was almost as destitute of funds as when he started it.

Another significant dwelling in Revolutionary times was the Dillaway House in Roxbury (Page 165), then the parsonage of the First Church. The patriotic pastor turned it over to General John Thomas, who made it his headquarters. The house is located on a hill overlooking all of Boston, and it virtually became the Headquarters of the army during the Siege of Boston, as Generals Heath and Knox and many other officers witnessed from its windows the activities of the British, the Battle of Bunker Hill and the Evacuation.

Finally, a gambrel-roofed house of distinctly another sort is found in the Huguenot House in New London, for this is built entirely of stone, with plump chimneys at the ends (Page 165). It gets its name from the fact that it was built by Huguenot refugees for Nathaniel Hempstead, a descendant of Robert Hempstead, who received an original grant from James I. The house now serves as a Tea House and Bookshop.

Little did Joseph Webb realize, when he built himself a fine gambrel-roofed house in Wethersfield, Conn., in 1752 (Page 166), that his son would entertain George Washington there many times, and that it would be the scene of a famous conference between General Washington and Rochambeau. This meeting was held in the South Room, known as the Council Room, and resulted in a joint campaign of French and American forces which terminated the Revolution with the capture of Cornwallis at Yorktown. Washington's own bedroom is now preserved with its original wall paper. The Webb House is very handsome, with a well-proportioned facade and good window treatment. It has a spacious central hall marked with a well-carved staircase, and many of the rooms are finished with remarkably fine panelling. In the large attic is a gallery, and in one of the chimneys is a smoke room for curing hams and other meats. A charming garden has been planted behind the house.

It is something of a jump from here to the far elbow of Cape Cod, and the Atwood House, oldest in Chatham (Page 167). This serene old shingled homestead was a rarity in its day, for it had a gambrel roof, not the conventional pitch roof of most Cape Cod cottages. It was built by a deep sea captain who made long voyages to odd parts of the globe. The wing on the left was added, so the story goes, by one of his descendants, John Atwood, who had promised his bride a fine new house after their marriage. Instead he built this wing, and when his wife reminded him that a kitchen ell could hardly be a fulfillment of his promise, the ungallant bridegroom said, "That was only courtin' talk."

The Mayflower Society House in Plymouth (Page 167) holds a variety of interests. It was built in 1754 by Edward Winslow, grandson of the early Governor who came over on the *Mayflower*. The frame of the house, according to current belief, was brought over from England. In the east living room Ralph Waldo Emerson was married to Lydia Jackson, whose father owned the house at that time. The house is being furnished with Queen Anne and early Chippendale furniture. A superb view of Plymouth harbor can be obtained from its cupola.

It was on the roof of the Page House in Danvers (Page 168), that Madam Page's tea party was held, since they had agreed not to use tea under their roof. In a front room of this house General Page maintained his private office in 1774. When the Lexington alarm came to Danvers, Captain Jeremiah Page left the house to lead his company in a quick march to Lexington. Returning from the battlefield, the cart carrying the dead and wounded of Danvers stopped before the door.

A rare old brick house with a lean-to faces the town green in West Springfield. It is the Josiah Day House (Page 168), recently restored with care and good taste. None but members of the Day family, some of whom achieved great distinction in the business world, ever lived in the house. Early furniture graces the larger rooms, each of which rejoices in a huge fireplace.

On the site of the old Plymouth trading post, overlooking the Kennebec River in Augusta (Page 169), a fort was built in 1754 as a protection against the Indians. Behind its forbidding palisade were two blockhouses, a barracks, officers' quarters, store rooms and a parade ground. The blockhouses have now been rebuilt along the river bank while the original garrison house has been well restored, furnished with antiques and filled with relics for the benefit of summer visitors.

In the matchless little town of Stroudwater, Maine, near Portland, is a large house, each of whose eight central rooms has a fireplace opening into one enormous chimney. This is the Tate House (Page 169), built for the Crown Mast Agent, George Tate, whose son became an Admiral in the Russian Navy. Over the sitting room fireplace are two panels of "'illegal" width.

It is something of a jump from Maine to Barnstable, on Cape Cod, where the quiet Crocker Tavern welcomed weary stagecoach passengers for many a generation (Page 170). This is a simple old hostelry, without pretense but with decided charm and hospitality.

An ambitious New London dwelling in the maritime tradition is the Shaw Mansion (Page 170). It was built by the wealthy ship-owner, Captain Nathaniel Shaw, largely to give work to Arcadian peasants who blasted the rock away from the present site and built this somewhat austere house. Capt. Shaw's son, also Nathaniel, was prominent during the Revolution as Continental Naval Agent, and the house played an important official part throughout the war. Once it was set on fire, but the flames were quickly extinguished by loyal neighbors, with vinegar which was stored in kegs in the attic. Many distinguished men passed in and out of the mansion, and the room which George Washington occupied has been preserved in its original condition.

The sunny, gambrel-roofed house shown on Page 171 was the home of the first Commander-in-Chief of the American Navy, Esek Hopkins. In pre-Revolutionary days, when Rhode Island held a dominant place in shipping and privateering, Esek Hopkins was known as the ablest and most enterprising of all sea captains. Three of his brothers were also skippers and another brother was the statesman and Signer of the Declaration of Independence, Stephen Hopkins. The house is now used by Colonial and patriotic societies, and still retains Esek Hopkins' own furniture.

Another house with a nautical background is the John Paul Jones House in Portsmouth (Page 171), where the great admiral resided while fitting out the *Ranger* in 1777 and the *America* in 1781-2. The house was originally built by Gregory Purcell, a merchant sea captain who married Sarah Wentworth, niece of the celebrated Governor Benning Wentworth. Purcell died in 1776, leaving his widow to support her family of seven children by turning the house into a genteel boarding house. John Paul Jones was her most famous lodger. He is said to have spent his happiest days in Portsmouth, where he had many devoted friends.

The New England mansion reaches its most distinguished and harmonious form in the Longfellow House, a fine adaptation of English classic motifs to American conditions (Page 172). It was built in 1759 by Major John Vassall, an ardent Tory. Cambridge at that time was a favorite with rich Loyalists, who built many handsome, dignified estates in the town. Hostile demonstrations were frequently held outside this house, and in 1774 Major Vassall was driven out. He sailed for England in exile in 1778, and the estate was confiscated by Congress. At the outbreak of the Revolution it was occupied by Colonel Glover and his Marblehead troops. General Washington made it his headquarters from July, 1775 to April, 1776. His office was at the right, and the parlor at the left was Mrs. Washington's drawing room. Dr. Andrew Craigie owned the house by 1791. When Henry Wadsworth Longfellow came to Harvard as Professor of English in 1837, he took rooms at the Craigie House, with several other brilliant young men. After his marriage in 1843 he occupied the whole house, until his death in 1882. During the years that he lived here he wrote the great majority of his poems. The house is now occupied by his descendants. Architecturally it introduces several innovations for that period, among them exterior pilasters and a pediment over the entrance motif.

The name of William Cullen Bryant has been lent to a house in Great Barrington, Mass., which is much older than the poet (Page 173). In the handsome old dwelling now located in the grounds of the Berkshire Inn, the young poet, then 26, courted Frances Fairchild. Here they were married, and lived for several years. General Burgoyne had been an honored guest in the house many years before. Exceptionally fine doorways and window casements grace the exterior.

Not many houses in New England can keep pace with the Longfellow House, but the Wentworth-Gardner House in Portsmouth is able to do so, at least from an architectural point of view (Pages 173-175). This house has details of extraordinary refinement, inside and out. It may truly be called a museum piece, having once been the property of the Metropolitan Museum of Art. It is built on the classic central-hall plan, with hipped roof, two chimneys, four rooms per floor and a small ell in the rear. The wide hallway is a dominant feature of the house, and is accented by the magnificent main portal, a copy of the original. It is a question whether a finer doorway design can be found in New England. The fifteen panelled door and the pineapple ornament are but two of the details which contribute to its beauty. The pedimented window frames are also most unusual in detail. Inside are some superlative examples of panelling and wood carving.

One of the rare titled ladies to insist upon using her title after the Revolution was the widow of the soldier-merchant, Sir William Pepperell. Lady Pepperell lived in her elaborate Georgian house at Kittery Point, (Page 176), until her death, always demanding the deference she thought was due her. The house is a most unusual one, with four chimneys, a hip roof, corner quoins and a striking center pavilion. Its interior was badly damaged by fire recently, but it has been restored with extraordinary skill.

A recent and welcome recruit to the open houses in York County, Maine, is "The Former Public House of Capt. Samuel Jefferds" in York Village (Page 177). Some noble rescue work has brought this estimable old tavern back to its pre-Revolutionary appearance, and it has been furnished with appropriate good taste. Its dark red clapboards, wide shingled roof and square brick chimney are precisely in the atmosphere of 1760, when it flourished as an inn.

Also restored within recent years is a massive, weathered house in the sylvan village of Boxford (Page 177). This was once the home of the Reverend Elizur Holyoke, great-grandson of the man for whom Mt. Holyoke was named, and nephew of the President of Harvard College. Some interesting period costumes and a collection of dolls are among the exhibits.

Another wayside inn rich in atmosphere is Merrell's Tavern in South Lee (Page 178). This weather-beaten veteran in the Berkshires somehow stirs the imagination. The tavern must have prospered, for a third floor obviously became necessary. Instead of continuing the brick structure up another floor, the work was done in wood, adding greatly to its picturesqueness. The kitchen wing has a touch of the old South. Inside is the original tap room and bar, and much of its early furniture.

One's imagination is genuinely stirred by the unique "Ocean Born Mary" House in Henniker, N. H., ("The only Henniker in the world"). It is necessary to motor up a dusty side road to reach this unique hillside structure, (Page 178), but most visitors will find the effort well spent. The place abounds with legends of the most fantastic sort, based on the fact that, two centuries ago, a baby was born on an emigrant ship while it was in the hands of pirates. At the request of the chief of the pirates, the baby was named Mary. Then the ship proceeded to Portsmouth. Later the pirates sent gifts to the baby, among them a piece of colored silk which the pirate chief requested be kept for Mary's wedding dress. Years later, at the time of her marriage to James Wallace, Mary's gown was indeed made from this silk. The couple then moved to Henniker and built this fine hip-roofed house on the hilltop. A piece of the silk from the wedding dress is carefully preserved in the house. Widow Mary Wallace died in her 94th year and is buried in the Quaker cemetery nearby.

The period of the 1760's was an era of prosperity, good craftsmanship and excellent taste, and some of our finest houses came from this all too brief epoch. The Richard Derby House in Salem (Pages 179, 180) is a notable example. Built at the head of the famous Derby Wharf, it is the oldest brick house in Salem, a gambrel-roofed veteran which is now fairly well surrounded by the city's Polish quarter. The beauties of the house are most apparent in the interiors. The panelling is of the very best. Simple bolection mouldings frame the fireplaces, and the interior casements are masterpieces of fine carpentry. The handsome stair rail will give an idea of the dexterity of those early craftsmen. Unfortunately the beautiful, soft color schemes cannot even be suggested by black-and-white pictures. The original paint colors have been matched in each room, and in John Derby's chamber the old tea box paper has been duplicated for the wall coverings. Many of the handsome furnishings came directly from the Derby descendents. Captain John Derby, son of the builder, also lived in this house. To him fell the rare distinction of taking the news of Lexington to London in advance of the Government, a fact which somehow seems startling in these days of radio communication. Again in 1783 he was the first to bring home news of peace, having sailed with the tidings from Paris on the ship *Astrea*. The house was rescued from oblivion in 1927 by the Society for the Preservation of New England Antiquities, and donated to the Government in 1937.

When John Hicks, a carpenter by trade, built his own house in Cambridge in 1762, he little imagined that it would one day serve as a house library for Harvard students (Page 181). The house has other distinctions. Once it was commandeered by General Washington and General Putnam for the use of their subordinate officers, and for the storage of supplies. The son of John Hicks, the builder, was an ardent patriot who joined the Boston Tea Party by letting himself down from the north bedroom window by a sheet rope.

The name of Grinling Gibbons, the celebrated English wood carver, has been associated loosely with many American houses. One of the few which really can lay claim to possessing his carving is the noble Moffatt-Ladd House in Portsmouth (Pages 182, 183). The spacious hallway of this mansion is without a parallel in New England. It is embellished with the famous "Bay of Naples" picture paper printed by Joseph Dufour in Paris around 1815. The panelling is elaborate and the furnishings are exquisite throughout this remarkable mansion. Adjoining it are an old Counting House and Coach House, both recently restored. The old fashioned garden is an added joy.

The morning sunlight caresses the silvery shingles of the old Thomas Cooke House in Edgartown, the metropolis of Martha's Vineyard (Page 184). It is a commodious house with a whitewashed central chimney, built without frills and well equipped to resist salty weather.

A mansion in every sense of the word is the imposing residence which Colo nel Jeremiah Lee, the prominent merchant, built for himself in Marblehead in 1768 (Pages 185, 186). It was said to be one of the most expensive houses in the British Colonies. Two magnificent sets of paper hangings were made especially for it in England. Its stairs were superbly carved, and its panelling and wood carving, inspired by measured drawings from England, was of the finest. The whole house is massive in scale, delicate in detail. It contains much interesting furniture and a large collection of historical relics.

When Judith Sargent married John Murray, founder of Universalism, in Gloucester, she received as a wedding present from her father an imposing house overlooking Gloucester Harbor (Page 187). Besides the interest of personalities, the house is filled with interior woodwork of extraordinary refinement. The staircase is most elaborate, as are the mantels in the parlors. In addition to many fine period pieces, there are some good portraits, including the work of John Singer Sargent, a descendant of the builder. The Rev. Samuel Gilman, author of "Fair Harvard" was born here in 1791.

(At this point, the author would like to digress for a moment and to express particular regret for not having taken photographs of another estate in the Gloucester district which offers an extraordinary opportunity to lovers of antiquity. This is the remarkable "Beauport" on Eastern Point Boulevard, Gloucester, a modern structure, with a most incredible collection of antiquities, complete rooms and separate pieces. It is the most outstanding of the many properties of the Society for the Preservation of New England Antiquities, and is described in the Check List in Chapter II.)

The cheerful Old Constitution House in Windsor, Vermont (Page 187), owes its name to the fact that the Vermont Constitution was drawn up and signed within its walls in 1777. It was also used for the first session of the state legislature. At that time it was a tavern, and had probably been constructed about five years earlier. The building is rich in relics and documents relating to the early history of Vermont.

Among Old Deerfield's notable houses are several owned by Deerfield Academy and open to visitors. The Old Manse (Page 188), is one of them. This is definitely a square house, one facade differing from the other only in the elaboration of the doorway. The original doors, knockers and boot-scrapers have come down from 1768, and there is much fine wallpaper and furniture inside. The house once served as an underground railroad depot for fugitive slaves.

Another Old Manse of extraordinary interest is in Concord (Page 188), within a hundred yards of historic North Bridge. Built by the Reverend William Emerson in 1769, it has undergone amazingly little change since that time. Save for a span of four years when Nathaniel Hawthorne lived in the house and made it known to the world by his "Mosses from an Old Manse," it was occupied by relatives or descendants of William Emerson until 1934. Set well back from the road in serene privacy, the Manse is rich in the atmosphere of 18th Century New England, save for the central dormer, which was added in 1846. There are many intimate souvenirs in the Manse: inscriptions on the window panes by Hawthorne and his bride, pencilled notations by Ralph Waldo Emerson (here he wrote "Nature"), and a superb library of books, old and new. The house is also rich in memories of the brilliant Mrs. Sarah Bradford Ripley, who returned to the house in 1846, after Hawthorne's departure, and tutored the Harvard students in French, German, Italian, Latin, Greek and Hebrew, regretting that though she could read Sanscrit, she could not speak it. She specialized in higher mathematics; was much interested in astronomy, botany, chemistry, history and philosophy, had seven children and said that the finest thing she could do was to make a pie her husband really enjoyed!

An agreeable little gambrel-roofed dwelling, far from the turmoil of the Revolution, is the Historical House in Wallingford, Conn., known also as the Samuel Parsons House (Page 189). Its very discreet dormers and well designed little entrance porch set it off from the more severe cottages of earlier periods.

The fine old Burnham Tavern in Machias (Page 189) was built seven years after the first settlers landed in the village, and is the only building in Eastern Maine with a Revolutionary record. A band of volunteers met in this house in 1775 and laid the plans which culminated in the capture of the British frigate *Margaretta*. This engagement has been appropriately termed "the Lexington of the Seas." After this battle the Burnham Tavern was turned into a hospital for the wounded, and here Captain Moore of the *Margaretta* was brought, mortally wounded. The chest on which he was laid is still to be seen in the Tavern, with stains which are supposed to be his blood. In every room of this house will be found relics of historic interest.

Nathanael Greene, a young Quaker whose father owned a prosperous forge and foundry in Warwick, R. I., was chosen from among eight brothers to take charge of the branch iron works in Anthony. Here in 1770 he built a neat two-story house with a wide central hall and a sweeping view of the valley below (Page 190). And here, four years later, he brought his bride. The story might have run along in this same uneventful fashion but for the Revolution, which skyrocketed Nathanael Greene into the High Command of the Army, second only to General Washington, who came to depend upon him more and more as the campaign wore on. Several rooms have been restored and furnished, much as they were in the General's day.

Half hidden by vegetation is the little red and white Betsey Williams Cottage in Providence (Page 190). A wisteria of gargantuan proportions has practically woven a web about this old gambrel-roofed homestead. During the time it is in blossom the house presents an unforgettable picture. Betsey Williams, a great-great-great-grand-daughter of Roger Williams, willed the land on which her cottage stands to the City of Providence, with the provision that it be called Roger Williams Park. The cottage contains furniture and relics relating to the early history of Rhode Island.

Few villages are as distinguished and well groomed as Litchfield, Conn. Its broad streets are lined with towering trees and stately mansions, among them the Tapping Reeve House (Page 191). This is square and hip-roofed, with an unconventional facade and two large wings. Tapping Reeve was an eminent lawyer who began to give lectures in 1782 and soon attracted students from all parts of the country. Classes were held in a little white building on the grounds (Page 191). Aaron Burr was his first pupil, and also the brother of Mrs. Reeve, and the room he occupied while studying at the school has been preserved, as has Lafayette's room. Over a thousand students came to study with Tapping Reeve, whose law school was the first in the country. They came from every state in the Union, and literally hundreds of them rose to high judicial rank.

At the sylvan crossroads of South Berwick, Maine, is another square Colonial house, half hidden by vegetation, the picture of New England calm and repose. This is the birthplace of Sarah Orne Jewett, whose works of fiction enjoyed much popularity toward the end of the 19th Century (Page 192). The central hall of this house is truly exceptional, and the rooms are richly furnished. Each of the four large bedrooms has a mahogany four-poster. Sarah Orne Jewett's work desk, where many of her books were written, is still preserved, and there is a small hidden staircase in the house, running from cellar to attic.

At the time of its construction in 1776 the house now known as the East India House was said to be the largest in the district. It contained 26 rooms, 14 fireplaces and 7 exits (Page 192). A subsequent owner engaged Joseph McIntire, father of Salem's great architect-carver Samuel McIntire, to do the panelling. Samuel, then a lad of about 18, assisted his father at this time, and later built the front doorway himself.

The imagination is stirred by the sight of a pioneer homestead which some courageous settler has built far up in the hills. Such a place is the little white house which Eleazer Brown built near Adams, Mass., in 1778 (Page 193). Erected on a plateau and surrounded by mammoth elms and maples planted by Eleazer Brown about 1800, the house commands an inspiring view of Mt. Greylock and the Hoosic Valley.

A pioneer of a different sort was John Cabot, the merchant of Beverly. His impressive brick mansion is the soul of dignity and wealth, and reflects much of the Georgian tradition. Frankly a square, three-story house of brick, its window treatment has been studied with care. Two chimneys are eloquent of the fireplace arrangements beneath, and the "captain's walk" is well placed to observe the ships entering Beverly Harbor (Page 193).

Another unique edifice which has travelled on rollers to its present site is the Old Hadley Farm Museum in Hadley, Mass. (Page 194). This commodious barn has been moved to the center of the town, near the Old Meeting House, and converted into an effective museum for a most amazing collection of old farm implements and vehicles. There are stage coaches, horse rakes, flax hatchels, cow pokes, corn husk horse collars, old oaken buckets, blacksmith's bellows, cheese presses and smoke houses, to mention only a few. The front portal, which is not exactly in character with the rustic material within, is a copy, and a good one. Many doorways of this handsome pattern can be found along the Connecticut River valley.

Salem's great era of merchant and shipping prosperity resulted in more than clipper ships and bulging wharves. A priceless by-product was the Salem mansion. The fine estates on Chestnut and Essex and Federal Streets remain the most impressive reminders of those active days, long after the last clipper ship has disappeared and the famous Derby Wharf has crumbled. Of these noble three-story houses, none excels the Peirce-Nichols House (Page 195), in the matter of wood carving. Considered by many to be the masterpiece of Samuel McIntire, it may well be the finest wood house of its period and type in New England. Built in 1782 by Jerathmiel Peirce, wealthy East India merchant, it is the central hall type, having on each side two rooms separated by a chimney. The interior woodwork was finished in 1801, and is doubtless McIntire's finest work, particularly the celebrated East Parlor. The rare beauty and refinement of McIntire's most perfect work cannot well be described in words. It must be seen to be appreciated. An unusually fine type of Salem fence stands before the house, surmounted with the original urns designed by the great carver-architect.

In a category entirely its own is the New England Colonial Village in Storrowtown (West Springfield), Mass. (Pages 196, 197). The ambitious and difficult idea of assembling a perfect village of old buildings around a Common has been accomplished with entire success. The scene now comprises all of the more picturesque elements which made up the village of a century and a half ago, with none of the scars and disfigurements which the intervening years have so often inflicted. The buildings spring from different periods, and have been moved from far and wide, but the ensemble is unquestionably pleasing and soothing to souls seared by skyscrapers.

The Gilbert Homestead (built in 1794), a hip-roofed farmhouse of great charm, was moved from West Brookfield, Massachusetts. The miniature law office of Zachariah Eddy, friend of Daniel Webster, was built about 1806 and transported from Eddyville, Massachusetts. The "Old Potter House," ample home of Captain John Potter of Revolutionary fame, came from North Brookfield. The Captain, who shared the sufferings of Washington's troops at Valley Forge, built the house, largely with his own hands, after the Revolutionary War. The little red brick schoolhouse, crowned by an open cupola, was brought from Whatley, Massachusetts, and the old stone blacksmith's shop came from Chesterfield, New Hampshire. The central axis of the group accents the dignified meeting house originally built in Salisbury, New Hampshire, in 1834. Oldest house in the village is the gambrel-roofed Phillips House, built in 1767 and moved from Taunton, Massachusetts. A typical Town Hall has come from Southwick, Massachusetts, where it was built in 1822. Finally there is the delightful Atkinson Tavern and Store, straight from the hill town of Prescott, Massachusetts, and complete down to the granite hitching posts.

At the bend of a country road in the township of Franklin, New Hampshire, is a two room cottage where Daniel Webster first saw the light of day on January 18, 1782 (Page 198). His father, Captain Ebenezer Webster, was allotted 225 acres on this wood hillside after taking part in the invasion of Canada in 1759. First he contrived a log cabin, and later built this modest house, which contains some good Webster memorabilia and an old kitchen of interest.

The veneration which New England feels for Henry Wadsworth Longfellow is reflected in the number of old houses which have been preserved in his name. Besides the Wayside Inn and the mansion in Cambridge, two houses in Portland are dedicated to the poet. One of them is the Wadsworth-Longfellow House (Page 199). Surrounded by an old fashioned garden, it forms a peaceful interlude in the very heart of Portland's business district. The house was built by the poet's grandfather and originally had but two stories. A third floor was added in 1815 after a fire, and there are now 16 rooms and 8 fireplaces. The poet spent his boyhood and the greater part of his first 35 years here. His first poem was composed here, as well as "The Courtship of Miles Standish." The actual birthplace of the poet is a typical old Portland house (Page 198), which has been preserved by the International Longfellow Society, and which now contains a most comprehensive library.

Another house which has been preserved in honor of a man of letters is "Rokeby," in Ferrisburg, Vermont (Page 200), the home of Vermont's celebrated poet and illustrator, Rowland E. Robinson. The house is set high on a hill and contains many of the works and intimate surroundings of the author who, even after he became blind, continued to write, up until an hour of his death. The house was one of the stations of the "Underground Railroad" and has served as the Town Clerk's office since 1857.

One of the broadest and most beautiful village streets in America runs through Longmeadow, Massachusetts, and one of the noblest houses to face this sylvan avenue is the Richard Salter Storrs Parsonage, built in 1786 (Page 200). This smiling structure has a fine pitched roof with a slight overhang and a handsome double leaf doorway. Displayed within are some notable antiques and many articles belonging to Stephen Williams, "The Boy Captive of Deerfield," who became the first minister of Longmeadow.

The past decade has seen no more significant addition to the ranks of "open houses" than the stately John Brown House in Providence (Pages 201, 202). This elegant brick mansion was built in the Federal style by John Brown, merchant prince and one of the four celebrated Brown brothers of Providence. The house was designed by his brother, Joseph Brown. The cornerstone was laid in 1786, but it took two years to complete the massive house, which had four large rooms on each floor. George Washington visited the house in 1790 and drank a glass of punch with his admirer, John Brown. In those days it was the scene of brilliant social functions. In the dining room is a scenic wall paper which depicts Washington's inauguration in New York in 1789. The rooms on the first floor are handsomely furnished in the style of the period. Other rooms are given over to an extensive library and a notable collection of portraits, manuscripts, newspapers and genealogical records.

Along the broad Connecticut shore highways is a large white house whose commodious roof contains two attics, and whose sunny facade is most inviting. It is the Stanton House in Clinton (Page 202), standing on the site of Abraham Pierson's homestead, the old well of which still exists. The house is divided by a wide hall, and there is much beautiful panelling upstairs and down. The rooms occupied by Lafayette and Governor Buckingham have been preserved, and the house contains much fine china and furniture. The most noteworthy piece is a late 17th Century Court cupboard which was discovered in the barn of a neighboring farm. A one-story wing used to serve as a general store in Post-Revolutionary days, selling anything from molasses to tobacco, cowhide boots to calico. This store has been faithfully reproduced.

The elaborate two-story portico of the Julia A. Wood house in Falmouth (Page 203), sets it apart from most Cape Cod houses, which are inclined to be somewhat austere. The house, which was built shortly after the Revolution by Dr. Francis Wicks, is crowned by an authentic "captain's walk." From this eminence the anxious sea captain's wife could scan the horizon for sails.

Maria Mitchell, the first woman astronomer in America and a pioneer leader in the higher education for women, was born in a typical old Nantucket house with a "walk" on the roof (Page 204). It has now been dedicated as a memorial to this far seeing woman. The warm simplicity of the period furniture reflects the good taste of her home, where she lived for many years, adapting a part of the house for her astronomical observatory and scientific library.

A little pitch-roofed cottage adjoins the village green in North Andover (Page 204), and gives a very good idea of what a modest dwelling looked like at the end of the 18th Century. It is the North Andover Historical Society Cottage, built in 1796. Its whitewashed chimney shimmers and its trellised doorway welcomes the visitor, who will find the interior charmingly and appropriately furnished. Adjoining it is the well designed Samuel Dale Stevens Memorial Building, a museum containing, among other things, fine pewter, laces and Indian relics.

High Street, in Newburyport, is one of New England's most beautiful avenues, lined on either side with noble old houses of other centuries. One of these is the Pettingell-Fowler House (Page 205) which contains many reminders of the town's great shipping days.

A matchless opportunity to picture the surroundings of a patrician Boston household is afforded by the Harrison Gray Otis House, home of the distinguished statesman (Pages 206, 207). The house has been restored and furnished with the zeal and good taste of an archaeologist. The dignity, grace and luxury of a wealthy home in 1795 are revealed in an unforgettable manner. The mantels, which have an Adamesque grace, are exquisite, and the plan of the house is worked out so skillfully that, if it seems difficult to prove that Charles Bulfinch was the actual designer, the conception is surely worthy of him. This was the third Harrison Gray Otis House in Boston. It now serves as headquarters for the Society for the Preservation of New England Antiquities. In the rear is the Society's New England Museum, with a wide variety of interesting relics.

Built on quite as imposing a scale, but situated in the Maine countryside instead of the city, is "Montpelier," an accurate replica of the original 1795 residence of General Henry Knox, in Thomaston, Maine (Page 208). The famous Revolutionary general spent many of his years in Thomaston and died there. Much of the Knox furniture from the original structure has been preserved, and many other fine period pieces lend distinction to the interiors. The house is located on a hilltop and enjoys a sweeping view in all directions. The mansion contains an oval room graced by an elegant floor covering, a huge chandelier and portraits of Generals Washington and Knox. The "flying staircase" in the hall is very beautiful. The original house was demolished in 1871 when the railroad went through the town. The present brick railway station was one of the outbuildings of the estate. General Knox died in "Montpelier" in October 1806 as a result of swallowing a chicken bone.

The first settler of the little lakeside community of Naples, Maine, was Dr. George Pierce, "one of the fathers of New England colonization." Here he built a grist mill and a saw mill, and while he was at it, he built himself an impressive manor house on the hill (Page 208). It has brick ends, 24-paned windows and an elaborate doorway with reeded pilasters and a fine semi-circular top light. Above this is a Palladian window, making this quite an architectural jewel to be set among the Maine pines. "The Manor" is available to visitors who seek food and shelter as well as a glimpse of Dr. Pierce's architectural good taste.

The GOULDING HOUSE, built around the beginning of the 18th Century in South Sudbury, Mass., has been carefully restored with casement windows and fine panelling.

The PHINEAS UPHAM HOUSE, Melrose, Mass. (built 1703), grew from a two-room nucleus to amplitude and prosperity, and was rescued from a tattered old age in 1914.

The FISHER-RICHARDSON HOUSE, Mansfield, Mass. (built 1704), home of the first miller of Mansfield, is located near the Taunton bounds, surveyed by Miles Standish in 1640.

The DOROTHY QUINCY HOMESTEAD, Quincy, Mass., was built in 1706 around a nucleus said to date from 1636. It is one of the first "Colonial Mansions" in New England.

The STEPHEN HOPKINS HOUSE, Providence, R. I. (built 1708) was the home
of Stephen Hopkins, merchant and shipbuilder, ten times Governor of Rhode
Island and a Signer of the Declaration of Independence. George Washington was
a guest in this house April 6, 1776.

COUNT RUMFORD HOUSE, Woburn, Mass. (built 1714) is the birthplace of Benjamin Thompson, scientist and inventor, who was created a Count of the Holy Roman Empire and took the title of Count Rumford.

The WAYSIDE, Concord, Mass. (first part built about 1717) is celebrated as the home of four authors Nathaniel Hawthorne, Bronson Alcott, Louisa M. Alcott and "Margaret Sidney," author of "The Five Little Peppers."

"THE OLD CASTLE," Pigeon Cove, Mass., said to date from 1715, may have been built by the Town of Gloucester to shelter loggers who were sent to cut down the heavily timbered town lands.

"FRUITLANDS," Harvard, Mass. (built before 1717). Here it was that A. Bronson Alcott, the Transcendentalist, and the English Mystics tried to create a "New Eden" in 1843.

The SHAKER HOUSE, Harvard, Mass. (built 1781), is the oldest house erected by the Shakers at the Harvard Shaker Village. Recently it has been moved to this site on Prospect Hill.

The WARNER HOUSE, Portsmouth, N. H. (built 1718), with its fine doorway, dormers and "captain's walk," is the forerunner of many fine New England mansions. Benjamin Franklin placed a lightning rod on this house.

The most beautiful gate posts in America are to be found in Salem. This one, which stands sentinel before the ROPES MANSION, is a very subtle fragment of architecture, copied after McIntire.

The ROPES MANSION, Salem, Mass. (built 1719), gives an accurate picture of the life of a well-to-do family in the early 18th Century. It contains much fine furniture.

The ROPES MANSION, Salem, was the residence of a Tory family before the Revolution, and later the home of a typical prosperous Salem family during the town's great merchant period (1790-1830).

CINCINNATI HALL, Exeter, N. H. (built 1721) formerly known as the Ladd-Gilman House, was the birthplace of Nicholas Gilman, Jr., Signer of the Constitution. The house was used as the State Treasury during the Revolution.

The JUDSON HOUSE, Stratford, Conn. (built 1723), has rare overhanging gables and a twelve foot chimney which serves six fireplaces and supports heavy 18-inch beams.

The table is set in the panelled dining room of the JUDSON HOUSE, just as it might have been two centuries ago. The house is a veritable museum of Colonial furniture and objets d'art.

The CUDWORTH HOUSE, Scituate, Mass. (built 1723), is interesting as a typical gambrel-roofed homestead, with white trim, shingled sides and roof, and a substantial chimney.

The WADSWORTH HOUSE, Cambridge, Mass. (built 1726) the home of Harvard Presidents for 123 years, was occupied by Presidents Josiah Quincy, Edward Everett, Jared Sparks, James Walker and Cornelius C. Felton. George Washington used it for Headquarters in 1775.

The MARTIN HOUSE, Swansea, Mass., was built in 1728 on the site of a house burned by the Indians. Its architecture has the savor of neighboring Cape Cod.

"WHITEHALL," Middletown, R. I. (built 1729), was the American home of the celebrated philosopher, poet and divine, George Berkeley, Dean of Derry, afterwards Lord Bishop of Cloyne.

The OLD EGREMONT TAVERN, South Egremont, Mass., built in 1730 along the old Turnpike between Hartford and Albany, was used as a stopping place for stage-coach passengers.

The ADAMS MANSION, Quincy, Mass. (built 1731), was the home of Presidents John Adams and John Quincy Adams. John and Abigail Adams died here. In 1824 Lafayette paid a visit to John Adams here.

The PUTNAM COTTAGE, Greenwich, Conn. (built 1731?), was originally Knapp's Tavern. According to tradition, General Israel Putnam was staying at this tavern on February 26, 1779 and escaped from the advancing British by plunging down a steep precipice on his horse.

The ROYALL HOUSE, Medford, Mass., is built around an original farmhouse supposedly constructed by Governor Winthrop in the 1630's. The present Colonial "nobleman's house" dates from 1732.

The ROYALL HOUSE, Medford, has a formal facade fashioned in wood to resemble stone, and facing to the Northwest. Nearby is a brick building called the slave quarters, another rarity in New England.

The SHORT HOUSE, Newbury, Mass. (built 1733) is a two-story wooden house,
built between ends of brick, and still in a splendid state of preservation. Its fine
doorway is painted a dull red, as is the exterior trim. The clapboards are weathered
a dark brown.

The SHORT HOUSE, Newbury, is the possessor of early 18th Century panelled
woodwork which can be equalled by few houses in America.

The MISSION HOUSE in Stockbridge, Mass. (built 1739) contains one of the finest examples of a broken-pediment, double-leaf doorway to be found in this country. It was built for John Sergeant, the young tutor at Yale College who became the first missionary to the Housatonic Indians.

The BRATTLE HOUSE in Cambridge, Mass. (built about 1735) was the home of William Brattle, physician, preacher, lawyer and Brigadier General of the British Provincial troops.

The NATHANIEL ALLIS HOUSE, Madison, Conn. (built 1739) was once the home of Cornelius Bushnell, the ship owner whose vessels were used by the Government in the Civil War.

The TOBIAS LEAR HOUSE, Portsmouth, N. H. (built about 1740), is the birthplace of Tobias Lear, who became George Washington's private secretary, and who twice married nieces of Martha Washington.

The ELLSWORTH HOMESTEAD, Windsor, Conn. (built 1740) was the home of Oliver Ellsworth, Framer of the Constitution, third Chief Justice of the Supreme Court and Envoy Extraordinary to France.

The EDWARD DEVOTION HOUSE, Brookline, Mass. (built about 1740) is now
surrounded by a modern school, a reminder that Edward Devotion, the elder, was
one of the first to bequeath money to the Town for its schools.

The RYTHER HOUSE, Bernardston, Mass. (built 1745), contains some unique wall
paintings, said to have been painted by a British spy who remained in seclusion here
during the War of 1812.

The KING HOOPER MANSION, Marblehead, Mass., built by a merchant prince in 1745, is one of the more recent houses to be rescued and restored. In contrast to this picturesque rear wing, the front facade is dignified and formal.

The cedar kitchen of the KING HOOPER MANSION, dating from an earlier period than the formal front portion of the house, has all the primitive charm of the 17th Century.

A close-up of the weathered sides of the RICHARD MANSFIELD HOUSE, Ansonia, Conn., built in 1747 for the Reverend Mansfield, first Episcopal minister in the town, who served for 72 years.

Almost dwarfed by the Doric portico of the First Parish Church, the hip-roofed
WRIGHT TAVERN (built 1747) faces the church green in Concord, Mass. This
tavern served as the British headquarters on the 19th of April 1775 and it was here
that Major Pitcairn made his celebrated boast.

In the GILBERT STUART BIRTHPLACE, North Kingstown, R. I. (built about
1750), was born in 1755 one of America's great painters, son of Gilbert Stuart, Sr., the
snuff-grinder.

From the rear windows of the DILLAWAY HOUSE, Roxbury, Mass. (built 1750), Generals Heath and Knox, and other officers witnessed the siege of Boston and the Battle of Bunker Hill.

The HUGUENOT HOUSE, New London, Conn., built about 1751 for Nathaniel Hempstead by Huguenot refugees, is another rarity, a gambrel-roofed cottage constructed of stone.

The WEBB HOUSE, Wethersfield, Conn. (built 1752), is famous as the meeting place of Generals Washington and Rochambeau in 1781, when plans for the Yorktown campaign were perfected.

The ATWOOD HOUSE, Chatham, Mass., was built in 1752 by Joseph Atwood, "a navigator of unfrequented parts." It is the oldest, and aesthetically the most satisfying house in this old Cape Cod town.

The MAYFLOWER HOUSE in historic Plymouth, Mass. was built in 1754 by a grandson of Governor Edward Winslow, who crossed on the Mayflower. In this house Ralph Waldo Emerson was married.

The PAGE HOUSE, Danvers, Mass., was built in 1754 by Captain Jeremiah Page, a staunch patriot who went from this house at the head of his Company when the Lexington alarm sounded.

The JOSIAH DAY HOUSE, West Springfield, Mass. (built 1754), is one of the extremely rare "salt-box" houses to be built of brick. The chimney has unusual width.

FORT WESTERN, situated along the banks of the Kennebec River in Augusta, Maine, was built in 1754 as a protection against the Indians. The original garrison house has now been restored and contains many relics of interest.

The TATE HOUSE, Stroudwater, Maine (built 1755), has many unusual features, including a high gambrel roof, an unprecedented dormer window and an idyllic setting in a perfect Maine village.

The CROCKER TAVERN, Barnstable, Mass. (built 1754) was for years a wayside tavern. Travelers along Cape Cod's main highway were for years welcomed to this cheerful structure.

The SHAW MANSION, New London, Conn., was built in 1756 by Captain Nathaniel Shaw, wealthy ship owner. Washington was entertained here in 1776, and Nathan Hale was a frequent visitor.

The ESEK HOPKINS HOUSE, Providence, R. I. (built 1756) was the home of Esek Hopkins, first Commander-in-Chief of the American Navy, and brother of the illustrious Stephen Hopkins.

The JOHN PAUL JONES HOUSE, Portsmouth, N. H. (built 1758), is celebrated as the home of Admiral John Paul Jones, who lived here while fitting out the "Ranger" in 1777.

THE LONGFELLOW HOUSE, Cambridge, Mass., was built in 1759 by Major John Vassal, a Tory, who was driven out of the house in 1774. The mansion served as Headquarters for General Washington from July 1775 to April 1776. Henry Wadsworth Longfellow occupied the house for 45 years, up to his death in 1882.

The WILLIAM CULLEN BRYANT HOUSE, Great Barrington, Mass. (built 1759), is the scene of the poet's courtship and marriage in 1821 to Miss Frances Fairchild, and his residence while serving as Town Clerk.

The WENTWORTH-GARDNER HOUSE, Portsmouth, N. H. (built 1760), looks across Portsmouth Harbor, and is sheltered by a magnificent linden. Its wooden facade is contrived in imitation of stone ashlar.

The doorway of the WENTWORTH-GARDNER HOUSE, Portsmouth, crested with its "pineapple" ornament, is one of the noblest designs in New England. The house is now owned by the Metropolitan Museum of Art.

The furnishings and wall coverings of the WENTWORTH-GARDNER HOUSE are in keeping with its architectural pre-eminence. The walls of its dining room have been enriched with an old English picture paper of classic design.

The LADY PEPPERELL HOUSE in Kittery Point, Maine (built in 1760) was the home of one titled lady who refused to consider that she had been deprived of her title by the Revolution. After a recent fire, the house has been carefully restored to its former state.

The old JEFFERDS' TAVERN in York Village, Maine (built in 1750), has been restored and furnished much as it was in the days of its former landlord, Captain **Samuel Jefferds.**

The large weathered HOLYOKE-FRENCH HOUSE in Boxford, Mass. (built in 1760), was once the home of the Reverend Elizur Holyoke, great-grandson of the man for whom Mt. Holyoke was named.

MERRELL'S TAVERN in South Lee, Mass. (built about 1760), is one of New England's most picturesque hostelries. A wooden third floor has been added to the original two-story brick tavern.

A good deal of imaginative folklore, embracing pirates and a new born babe, has sprung up in regard to the OCEAN BORN MARY HOUSE, built about 1760 on a hilltop above Henniker, N. H.

The DERBY HOUSE, Salem, Mass. (built 1762), is the oldest brick house in Salem, (center). Its panelled interiors are among the finest that exist from this period of unusual good taste.

The interiors of the DERBY HOUSE, the best of their epoch in Salem, are eloquent in their use of color and deep-cut mouldings. The house is now the property of the United States Government.

The skill of Salem's early wood carvers is evident in the beautiful, baffling and complex stair rail in the DERBY HOUSE. The casement windows are also extraordinarily fine.

The JOHN HICKS HOUSE, Cambridge, Mass. (built 1762), was used as an Army office by General Putnam during the Revolution, a fact which is almost belied by this peaceful facade. It is now the property of Harvard University.

The MOFFATT-LADD HOUSE, Portsmouth, N. H. (built 1763) is one of New Hampshire's most serene and imposing mansions. It is supposed to be a copy of Captain John Moffatt's boyhood home in Hertfordshire.

The interior of the MOFFATT-LADD HOUSE, Portsmouth, N. H., is enriched by superb wood carving, some of which is by Grinling Gibbons, and by a finely preserved "Bay of Naples" wall paper, printed by Joseph Dufour in Paris about 1815.

The venerable **ESQUIRE THOMAS COOKE HOUSE**, built 1766 in Edgartown, Mass., is typical of many weather-beaten, silver-shingled white-trimmed houses on Martha's Vineyard.

184

The LEE MANSION, Marblehead, Mass. (built 1768), is said to have cost its prosperous owner ten thousand Pre-Revolutionary pounds. Washington, Lafayette and Andrew Jackson were all entertained here.

The many imposing rooms of the LEE MANSION, Marblehead, contain some fine panelling. Other rooms still have their old wall papers intact, most of which were imported from England.

There are few, if any, examples of Grinling Gibbons type of wood-carving in America which equal this specimen in the LEE MANSION, Marblehead. It is flawlessly preserved.

The SARGENT-MURRAY-GILMAN-HOUGH HOUSE, Gloucester, Mass., was
built in 1768 by Winthrop Sargent, as a wedding present for his daughter Judith, who
married John Murray, founder of Universalism in America.

The OLD CONSTITUTION HOUSE, Windsor, Vermont (built about 1768?), was
the scene of the adoption of the Constitution of the State of Vermont in the year 1777.

The OLD MANSE, Old Deerfield, Mass. (built 1694, 1768), was one of the underground railroad depots for fugitive slaves. Emerson, Horace Greeley and Charles Sumner were visitors here.

The OLD MANSE, Concord, Mass. (built 1769), is but a stone's throw from historic North Bridge. Reverend William Emerson, builder of the house and grandfather of Ralph Waldo Emerson, watched the battle of April 19, 1775, from the study window. Nathaniel Hawthorne lived here for nearly four years.

The HISTORICAL HOUSE, Wallingford, Conn. (built 1770), is a gambrel-roofed cottage which appears to be an ancestor, with many refinements, of the contemporary "Dutch Colonial" house.

The only building in Eastern Maine with a Revolutionary record is said to be the old BURNHAM TAVERN, built in Machias, Maine, in 1770. It served as an emergency hospital after the capture of the British frigate *Margaretta*, whose captain was brought, mortally wounded, to one of the tavern rooms.

The NATHANAEL GREENE HOMESTEAD, Anthony, R. I., was built in 1770 by
Nathanael Greene, a young Quaker who was destined to become second in command
to General Washington of the Continental Army.

The BETSEY WILLIAMS COTTAGE, Providence, R. I. (built 1773), for years the
home of a descendant of the founder of Rhode Island, is now almost smothered by a
gigantic wisteria vine.

The TAPPING REEVE HOUSE, Litchfield, Conn., was built in 1773 by Judge Tapping Reeve, who founded the first regular law school in the country. Aaron Burr, his brother-in-law, was one of Tapping Reeve's first pupils.

In the small building at the left, Judge TAPPING REEVE established his law school. Three of his students became Supreme Court Justices; 26 became U. S. Senators and 90 were Congressmen.

The CAPTAIN JEWETT HOUSE, South Berwick, Maine (built 1774), is the birthplace of the noted authoress, Sarah Orne Jewett. It contains many fine interiors, furnished with pieces of the period.

The EAST INDIA HOUSE, Salem, Mass. (built 1706, remodeled 1774-1780), contains a wig room, two powder rooms and a Tory hide-out in one of the chimneys. A quadrille was given here for General Lafayette in 1824.

The ELEAZER BROWN HOMESTEAD, Adams, Mass. (built 1778), is a pioneer home, perched on a far hillside in the Berkshires, and commanding a magnificent view of the Hoosic Valley.

The CABOT HOUSE, Beverly, Mass. (built 1781), was the mansion of a wealthy merchant, and later a bank and insurance office. Lafayette was welcomed from its steps in 1824.

The **OLD HADLEY FARM MUSEUM**, Hadley, Mass. (built 1782) is a large remodeled barn, containing a collection of farm implements and furnishings. Its doorway is an approximation of a celebrated double front door in Hadley.

194

The **PEIRCE-NICHOLS HOUSE**, Salem, Mass. (built 1782) is an early example
of the work of Salem's great carver-architect, Samuel McIntire, and considered by
many to be his finest.

A NEW ENGLAND COLONIAL VILLAGE has been brought together and re-assembled around a village green in the grounds of the Eastern States Exposition, West Springfield, Mass.

The group of old buildings gathered together in West Springfield, Mass. forms an almost idyllic oasis, free from telephone poles, traffic lights and other scars of the 20th Century.

Included in the NEW ENGLAND COLONIAL VILLAGE are a church, a mansion, lawyer's office, town hall, red brick schoolhouse, blacksmith's shop, tavern, general store, Cape Cod cottage, farmhouse and a huge barn and outbuildings.

The atmosphere of the NEW ENGLAND COLONIAL VILLAGE is cordial and genuine. The buildings are of different ages, ranging from the Chesterfield Blacksmith Shop (1750), to the Salisbury Meeting House (1834).

In the hills above Franklin, N. H. is the BIRTHPLACE OF DANIEL WEBSTER, a two-room frame cottage which is maintained much as it was when a piercing-eyed baby was born here in 1782.

The LONGFELLOW BIRTHPLACE, Portland, Maine (built 1784), is rich in tribute to the great poet who lived here in his infancy. It contains an extensive library.

The WADSWORTH-LONGFELLOW HOUSE, Portland, Maine (built 1785-86).
Here the poet Longfellow spent most of his first 35 years, writing his first poem behind
these brick walls.

"ROKEBY," Ferrisburg, Vermont (built before 1784), was the home of Rowland E. Robinson, Vermont's celebrated author and artist. It was one of the stations of the underground railroad for Southern slaves fleeing to Canada.

The commodious STORRS PARSONAGE, (right), built in 1786, adjoins the Public Library and faces the broad village green at Longmeadow, Mass.

The rich Doric porch of the JOHN BROWN HOUSE, (built 1786), in Providence, R. I., gives more than a hint of the architectural richness to be found within. Once a center of social brilliance, the mansion was the scene of a reception for George Washington after his inauguration as President.

A garden view of the JOHN BROWN HOUSE gives an idea of its generous dimensions and does much to explain why two years were needed to complete its construction.

The JOHN A. STANTON MEMORIAL, Clinton, Conn. (built 1789), was erected on the site of an earlier house occupied by Abraham Pierson, first rector of Yale College. The east front room still has the original wall paper, made in Paris.

The JULIA A. WOOD HOUSE, Falmouth, Mass. (built about 1790), with an elaborate porch and a "captain's walk," lends a maritime touch to the village green. Inside are many relics of whaling ships and some fine old pictures.

In the MARIA MITCHELL MEMORIAL HOUSE, a typical off-center Nantucket dwelling built in 1790, the first woman astronomer in America carried out her experiments.

The NORTH ANDOVER HISTORICAL SOCIETY COTTAGE (built in 1796), gives an accurate idea of what a modest New England dwelling looked like toward the end of the 18th Century.

The PETTINGELL-FOWLER HOUSE, Newburyport, Mass. (built about 1792), is a characteristic house of the period when Newburyport was a bustling and prosperous seaport.

The HARRISON GRAY OTIS HOUSE, Boston, Mass. (built 1795) preserves the chaste setting of a patrician household of post-Revolutionary times with entire authenticity. It was the distinguished home of a distinguished man, lawyer, orator, Federalist leader, Member of Congress, Mayor of Boston and U. S. Senator.

Connected with the HARRISON GRAY OTIS HOUSE, Boston, is a Museum containing ship models, Shaker objects, weaving equipment, collections of glass, ceramics, costumes, silver, etc.

The **HARRISON GRAY OTIS HOUSE**, Boston, is at present the Headquarters of the Society for the Preservation of New England Antiquities. Authorities consider that Charles Bulfinch was probably the architect.

"MONTPELIER," Thomaston, Maine, is a replica of the original mansion (built 1795), which was the home of Major General Henry Knox. It contains much of the furniture and personal effects of the great Revolutionary soldier.

"THE MANOR" was built in 1799 in the little inland town of Naples, Maine, by Dr. George Pierce, an early colonizer endowed with unusually good architectural taste.

Open House in New England

Gore Place, Waltham, Mass.

v

Nineteenth Century Houses

This chapter begins with a celebrated house usually associated with the 19th Century, although it was assembled from two houses of a much earlier period. This is "Orchard House" in Concord, the much visited home of the Alcotts, which was fondly called "Apple Slump" by the famous Louisa May. The Alcotts lived in the house from 1857 to 1877, during which time the gifted authoress wrote a part of "Little Women." Most of the furnishings in the old house are original Alcott possessions. "Beth's" melodeon can still be seen, as well as many of the costumes which the girls wore in the plays they loved so to produce. "Amy's" original drawings are still preserved on the woodwork of her room. Bronson Alcott's study and the room where Louisa Alcott did her writing retain their homelike atmosphere and bring her writings to life with a strange poignancy. The School of Philosophy, founded by Bronson Alcott in 1879 and long a summer meeting place for American philosophers, is but a few steps away (Page 217).

The most exciting and significant newcomer to these pages is unquestionably Old Sturbridge Village, the wonderful "Living Museum and Crafts Center" which has been assembled in Sturbridge, Massachusetts, close to

Route 20 and not far from Worcester (Pages 218-220). This admirable undertaking, which has been under way for more than a decade, was opened to the public after the end of World War II. With great sympathy and historical accuracy, it portrays a New England town as it might have appeared in the early 19th Century. More than twenty historic buildings are grouped on these 500 acres of rolling countryside. Many of the old houses and shops have been moved from other localities. Miner Grant's General Store, a fascinating place filled with a conglomerate stock of country store articles, came from Stafford, Connecticut. The unpainted "half-gambrel" Stephen Fitch House was transported from Willimantic, Connecticut. Almost facing it across the green is the Solomon Richards House, a red "salt-box" whose massive Dutch barn, filled with old farm implements and carriages, came from Schoharie, New York. There is a delightful grist mill in operation, besides a brick schoolhouse and shops for the cobbler, gunsmith, clockmaker, blacksmith and cabinet maker. An old meeting house at the end of the green is one of the most recent additions. The idea of Old Sturbridge Village grew from the original collection of "primitive" antiques brought together by Mr. Albert B. Wells and Mr. J. Cheney Wells' collection of early American clocks. These collections, amazing in their completeness, are everywhere evident in the Village. The recently completed Inn serves admirably as a museum for many of the pieces. The Village is a non-profit educational institution, with an active crafts program supplementing its value as a visual exhibit.

The modest old Baxter House in Gorham, Maine, welcomes visitors to view its collection of early relics of the town. It has few architectural pretensions, but its hospitable warmth is evident (Page 221).

The General Gideon Foster House in Peabody (Page 221) is reminiscent of numerous dignified three-story houses built in New England in the early 19th Century.

A fine example of the imposing mansion of the early 1800's was built from plans drawn by Alexander Parris, one of the few Boston architects whose work could be said to rival Bulfinch's. This was the Sweat Mansion in Portland, a finely proportioned structure now occupied by the Portland Society of Art. That Parris was a consummate master of detail is proven by the superb central hall and staircase, and by the semi-circular entrance portal, surmounted by its Palladian window, a most skillful achievement (Page 222).

The crescendo in fine house building continued but for a few years, reaching its most impressive summit in Gore Place, Waltham (Pages 223-226), considered by many architects to be one of the few truly great houses in the United States. The splendid brick mansion, with its bow front and wide-stretched wings, looked out upon broad and peaceful acres, and formed an estate of a magnitude which could only be equalled by the great mansions of the South. Gore Place was quite in keeping with the distinguished career of its builder, Governor Christopher Gore, Revolutionary soldier, statesman and diplomat. Gore was chosen as Massachusetts Commissioner to ratify the Constitution with John Hancock and Samuel Adams. Washington appointed him the first District Attorney of the Commonwealth, and later he served as Governor, Representative in Congress and United States Senator. Sent to England as a Commissioner under the Jay treaty, he remained there eight years as Chargé d'Affaires. It was during his residence in England that he conceived the idea of his Waltham mansion, but whether he consulted an English architect, or commissioned Bulfinch or one of the American architects has never been determined. One thing is certain—Gore Place, built between 1802 and 1804, has much of the atmosphere of an English country estate of the period. Its rooms are spacious, high ceilinged and formal, and admirably suited to receive the dignitaries who visited the Governor from home and abroad. The State Reception Hall and the adjacent Oval Room could offer Lafayette and Tallyrand a setting quite in keeping with the salons they had known in Europe. Daniel Webster was a frequent visitor to Gore Place, but not in the ceremonial manner. For Governor Gore gave Webster his legal education, and three times dissuaded that brilliant man from giving up the legal career which later led him to such triumphs.

For a century Gore Place was carefully preserved in private hands, but subsequently it passed to other owners, and became successively an automobile agency, a country club and a road house. Following foreclosure proceedings the mansion narrowly escaped being torn down, while its broad acres were threatened with subdivision into building lots. The property was saved by the timely and energetic action of a few appreciative citizens. Public and private subscriptions have aided the cause, and a great deal of superb furniture has been loaned to furnish the house in something of the splendor it once knew.

American domestic architecture is fast reaching its peak with the Pingree House in Salem, conceived in the full maturity of Samuel McIntire's creative career (Pages 226-229). Its portal and exterior proportions are executed with great delicacy and sense of scale, and somehow succeed in expressing an atmosphere of restrained opulence which characterized the old Salem families. But the interiors once again show the carver-architect at his best. Such a simple thing as a door or a mantel can reveal the difference between a mere craftsman and a master such as McIntire. In the Pingree House, which has been magnificently furnished in the spirit of a wealthy merchant's home, he is at his best, which is an eminent pinnacle indeed. This brick mansion was built in 1804 for a prosperous sea captain, John Gardner. Thirty years later it was sold to David Pingree, in whose family it remained until it was conveyed to the care of the Essex Institute. Several of the original McIntire mantels had been replaced by marble ones during the Victorian era. Luckily the originals had been stored in the attic, and have been put back where McIntire installed them. The house is now flawlessly furnished. No detail has been overlooked in bringing it back to its unquestioned position as one of the truly great houses in America.

The best Georgian house in the State of Vermont, according to many critics, is "Grassmount," in the college town of Burlington (Page 230). It was originally called "Grasse Mount" in honor of Comte de Grasse of Revolutionary fame. At one time it was the home of Governor Van Ness and the center of official entertaining. During this time it was the scene of a reception to General Lafayette, who had come to lay the corner stone on one of the college buildings. The house contains a fine carved stairway and nine delicately carved marble mantels, all imported from Italy.

Also associated with a famous name is the little white cottage in the hills of North Oxford, Mass., the birthplace of a noble woman, Clara Barton, Founder of the American Red Cross (Page 230). A desk used by her during the Civil War can be seen among the family relics. A summer camp for diabetic little girls is operated on the property in her memory.

The varied and paintable shore line of Gloucester, teeming with fishing boats, artists and net-menders, is so full of fascination that the visitor often overlooks some of the old tree-lined residential streets of the seaport. This is unfortunate, because some distinguished houses await inspection, one of the most interesting being the Cape Ann Historical House (Page 231). This three-story house with a cheerful, unpretentious facade, contains many things which recall the careers of the old-time sea captains. There are rooms fitted as only a sailor would fit them, and there are ship models, old china and marine souvenirs which are salty and reminiscent in the extreme.

In an open clearing overlooking the broad Sheepscot River near North Edgecomb, Maine, is a house of quite a different character. This is Fort Edgecomb, an octagonal blockhouse built of massive ash and pine timbers, and held together with husky pegs (Page 232). There are slits for musket fire on the ground floor and squared portholes for heavier armament on the overhanging second floor. A narrow lookout caps the picturesque structure, built in the troublesome years of 1808-1809 but never used in an engagement.

For many years travelers along the turnpike used to spend the night in a dignified brick tavern in the superbly picturesque one-street village of Hancock, New Hampshire (Page 232). The tavern was almost square, with four chimneys, a low hip roof and rooms which must have appeared as hospitable then as they do now. During the summer months it is open to visitors, who can admire its notable collection of lustre-ware, china and old furniture.

The Antiquarian House in Plymouth (Page 233) begins to show the grace and delicacy of the second Classic revival. Its octagonal plan reveals the influence of Thomas Jefferson's designs, which were then much copied. The house is rich in exhibits, among them some early 19th Century costumes and children's toys of great interest.

An architectural jewel of unexpected refinement is found in the far away village of Columbia Falls, Maine (Page 233). This is the cheerful little Ruggles House, built in 1810 for the prosperous lumber dealer, Judge Thomas Ruggles. The exterior trim of this house is surprisingly delicate and the detailed interior woodwork, carved by an unknown English artisan, is truly remarkable. Rich mahogany inlaid panels were uncovered during a recent restoration.

A strong possessive urge strikes many a passing motorist as he slows down for the village of Templeton, Massachusetts, on Route 2. There is something about this serene old house facing Templeton Common, something about its 30-paned windows, white panelled shutters and whitewashed brick chimneys which personifies the cherished dream of countless home seekers. Yet the house was built to be used as a store, and for decades it served as the village Postoffice and unofficial gathering place of the town patriarchs. Today it is the home of the Narragansett Historical Society (Page 234). The old country store room, complete with cracker barrel, cheese box and rotund stove, is still there, with the Postoffice pigeon-holes in the corner. The drug corner still uses Latin names exclusively. The "keeping-room" for the parson and the weaving room with a fine loom are just as they always have been. In the rear is a charming old fashioned garden where tea is served on summer Saturdays. The temptation to stop at this inviting spot will, if followed, bring a rich reward.

Similar in many ways to the Templeton house, and with the same simplicity and good taste, is the square brick house built by Samuel Fowler in Danversport (Pages 234, 235). Fowler was seventh in descent from Philip Fowler who settled in Ipswich in 1634, and he built substantially and well. The result is a house in an almost flawless state of preservation, even to the old festooned wall paper. There are four rooms on the ground floor and five above. The mantels, cornices, dadoes and panelled shutters are beautifully carved in restrained patterns. The chimneys are incorporated in the brick walls.

The color and romance of the Orient are woven into the imposing square house with the double deck porch in Providence (Page 236). This is the Carrington House, home of a very successful merchant in the China trade. It was originally a traditional two-story Federal house, but Edward Carrington added another story when he bought it in 1812. Mr. Carrington had spent nine years in China representing his shipping firm, and he returned with a love of things Chinese which is evident in every room of this most unusual house. The furnishings are of many periods, the Oriental objects being particularly fine. The private office of the merchant prince, where he received his sea captains and listened to their reports, is full of the atmosphere of old clipper ships.

It is not surprising that the natives of Winsted, Conn., upon seeing the many-columned estate which Solomon Rockwell built for himself and family in 1813, gave it the name of "Solomon's Temple" (Page 237). Built at a time when the classic revival had not become too corrupted, it gives an excellent example of two kinds of portico, one supporting a flat roof, the other a pediment. The builders paid great attention to carved details, inside and out. The mantels and woodwork were supposed to have been carved with a jack knife, and the detail of the barn and cabin make them gems of Federal architecture.

One of the best known 19th Century architects in the Connecticut Valley was Isaac Damon, who is credited with designing several distinguished churches and public buildings in the Northampton region. The simple house which he built for himself in 1812 can be seen during the summer months (Page 238). The architect's drafting implements and models of his work are exhibited, as well as a notable group of Jenny Lind articles.

"Buttonwoods" in Haverill (Page 238), resembles the Fowler House in some ways. This brick-end house of smiling countenance adjoins the old John Ward House, and is erected on the site of a house built long ago by the Rev. Ward for his daughter, then about to become Mrs. Saltonstall. Adjoining the house is a small museum with many historic relics. In the grounds of "Button-woods" is an ancient oak, its age going back indeterminate centuries, which may well be one of the oldest living things in New England.

The youngest of Portsmouth's many "open houses" is celebrated as the boyhood home of Thomas Bailey Aldrich, who immortalized that period, more or less, by writing the "Story of a Bad Boy." The house is correctly furnished in the style of 1840, and is rich in memorabilia of the noted author (Page 239).

If the Black Mansion in Ellsworth Maine (Page 239) is impressive to-day, it must have appeared fabulous when it was built in a tiny frontier settlement in the early 1800's. Colonel John Black, a land agent, was the owner of the house and lavished a fortune upon it. Its notable curving stair-case is worth seeing, as is an old Dutch chair which can be converted into a bed. There is also fine miniature of George Washington on exhibit. The grounds of the mansion are commodious and beautiful.

A typical New England mansion of the early 1800's is the Deacon Amos Blanchard House in Andover (Page 240). Its mantels and stair rails are finely carved, and the Deacon's carefully kept account books tell exactly the cost of everything that went into the house. Total cost, $4100.

Concord assumed its literary importance when Ralph Waldo Emerson took up his residence in 1835 in a comfortable white house (Page 241), after spending much of his youth in the Old Manse. Other writers followed, to form the "Concord Group," most important of their time in America. The house is now surrounded by pines which were planted by the philosopher himself. To it came people of all stations of life and all temperaments, to talk with the man whose philosophical writings had had such widespread effect. The house remains much as it was in Emerson's time, but the priceless contents of his study, with its books, manuscripts and pictures, have been installed in the fireproof building of the Antiquarian Society across the way.

The distinguished Trask House in Manchester (Page 241) preserves a certain nautical character, which very much belongs to this picturesque old town on the North Shore.

John Greenleaf Whittier lived in Amesbury, Massachusetts, for some 56 years, most of them in the simple white house behind its picket fence illustrated on Page 242. Most of his better known poems were written here, and the Garden Room, in which he wrote, has been kept as it was in his lifetime. Nearby is the Friends Meeting House which Whittier attended.

The spacious Blaine Mansion in Augusta, Maine, was built in the mood of the Classic Revival about 1830 (Page 243). In 1862 it was purchased by James G. Blaine, "the plumed knight of politics." Here he learned of his nomination for the Presidency, and here he received the news of his defeat in 1876. The house was presented to the State by his daughter in 1919, and it now serves as the Executive Mansion. Blaine's study remains as it was in his political prime. In the State Dining Room is a silver service which was recovered from the cruiser *Maine* ten years after it had been sunk in Havana Harbor.

A mansion of even greater dignity was built in Worcester about the same time by Stephen Salisbury, 2nd, member of a noted Massachusetts family (Page 243). The architect of this house, Elias Carter, interpreted classic forms with severe but remarkably good taste for the period. The house was bequeathed to the Worcester Art Museum in 1905 and was used as its art school for nearly 20 years. It has since been given to the Worcester Chapter of the American Red Cross, which uses it as a headquarters.

What a contrast between the Doric pomp of the Salisbury Mansion and the humble interior of the Lye Cobbler Shop in Salem! This small building, located in the grounds of the Essex Institute, is preserved exactly as it was more than a century ago, even to the scraps of leather on the floor (Page 244).

Another glimpse of early New England industry is furnished by the Spaulding Grist Mill in Townsend Harbor, Massachusetts (Page 244). Its venerable wooden and wrought iron machinery is still sound. Directly across the road from the Grist Mill is the Spaulding Cooperage Shop. Both of the buildings are owned by the Society for the Preservation of New England Antiquities, and both have been utilized by a very successful handicrafts program for children in recent years.

In the courtyard of Wiggins Old Tavern in Northampton, Massachusetts, is a country store which will produce a nostalgic effect on many visitors (Page 245). The typical country store has been faithfully rebuilt here, and its wandering interior is filled with an incredible miscellany of homely objects which used to be sold in a rural Yankee emporium. Another room is given over to weaving on an ancient loom, and yet another is devoted to antique furniture. The country store idea is well received in New England. The one in Concord has already been mentioned. There is a notable one called the

Vermont Country Store in Weston, Vermont, and another in Beverly, Massachusetts, goes under the name of "Johnny Appleseed's."

Inasmuch as the houses in this book are listed chronologically, the notable Antiquarian House in Concord (Pages 245, 246) technically comes last on the list, and permits this chapter to close in a blaze of glory. The house was built in 1929. Attempts to ascribe a date to its interior are useless, however, for it was constructed to shelter fifteen authentic period rooms dating from the middle 1600's up to the time of Emerson and Thoreau. The archaeological significance of these rooms is great, for they have been assembled and furnished with scrupulous accuracy and good taste. That utmost rarity, a pine-ceiled room, is found here. In the Seventeenth Century Room is something almost as unusual, an early American Oak Press Cupboard. There is a Green Room showing the impulse of the Renaissaince, a lovely Queen Anne Room and a Chippendale Room of rare charm. A Revolutionary Bedroom, a McIntire Room and a Reeded Room from about 1800 are followed by two simple exhibits which evoke the memory of two of Concord's greatest names. One of these is the bare little Thoreau Room, containing the furnishings of the hut at Walden Pond where Henry Thoreau lived and wrote. The other is the study of Ralph Waldo Emerson, exactly as the great philosopher left it. The identical room was first reproduced in these fireproof quarters and then the entire contents of the poet's study were moved here from the Emerson House across the way. In addition to these treasures are a Diorama of the Concord Fight, a memorable herb garden and, finally, one of the two lanterns which swung from the tower of the Old North Meeting House on the night of the ride of Paul Revere. Decidedly the Antiquarian House provides a fitting climax to the engrossing theme of Open House in New England.

"ORCHARD HOUSE," Concord, Mass., was assembled from two houses dating about 1650 and 1730 by Bronson Alcott in the 19th Century. It was here that Louisa May Alcott wrote the first part of "Little Women."

OLD STURBRIDGE VILLAGE, near Sturbridge, Mass., accurately portrays a New England country town as it might have appeared in the early 19th Century. Here is the shop of an old-time cabinet maker, John S. Moodie.

Miner Grant's General Store in OLD STURBRIDGE VILLAGE is an unpainted gambrel roof veteran with a broad front and back porch at different levels. It is filled with a fascinating miscellany of items which could be found in a country store a century or more ago.

The Solomon Richardson House in OLD STURBRIDGE VILLAGE is a red and white "salt-box" in the best Connecticut tradition. Adjoining it is a venerable barn filled with old farm equipment and vehicles.

The tiny shop of "Jesse Hitchcock, Shoe and Boot Maker" is one of the more nostalgic exhibits scattered over the 500 acres which comprise OLD STURBRIDGE VILLAGE.

Fine white corn meal is ground between two pairs of ancient mill stones in the Grist Mill of OLD STURBRIDGE VILLAGE. Water from the mill pond turns the twenty-foot undershot mill wheel.

The commodious Blacksmith Shop at OLD STURBRIDGE VILLAGE is filled with homely implements of the trade and many old carriages and sleighs. In the little white Blacksmith House is a fine display of old ironwork.

The BAXTER MUSEUM, Gorham, Maine (built about 1800), has been converted into a museum filled with early relics of the town's history.

The GENERAL GIDEON FOSTER HOUSE, Peabody, Mass. (built 1800), is interesting, not because it is exceptional, but because it is typical of hundreds of houses which were built near Boston at the beginning of the 19th Century.

The L. D. M. SWEAT MANSION, Portland, Maine, was built in 1800 from plans drawn by the Boston architect, Alexander Parris. Its ambitious entrance is deftly designed.

GORE PLACE, Waltham, Mass. (built 1802-4) is considered by architects to be one of America's few truly great houses. It was built by Christopher Gore, patriot, lawyer, First District Attorney of Massachusetts, Chargé d'Affaires in London and Governor of the Commonwealth. The spacious grounds once comprised eighty acres of land and three ponds. Few, if any, country estates in New England existed on such a large scale.

The central motif of GORE PLACE, Waltham, has an imposing bulge, flanked by two simple wings. The construction is brick throughout. Despite intensive research, the name of the architect remains uncertain.

There are many handsome bedrooms in GORE PLACE. In the Governor's bathroom was a huge lead tub and above it an opening in the ceiling which permitted his servants to pour warm water upon him, probably the first shower bath in America!

The subtle curves of the doorway leading to the Oval Room of GORE PLACE can easily be detected. Here the great governor entertained Tallyrand, Lafayette, Adams, Monroe, Daniel Webster and many another noted guest.

The stable and coach house of GORE PLACE possibly antedate the mansion itself.
The whole estate, house and all, recently had a narrow escape from destruction at the
hands of the real estate sub-dividers.

The PINGREE HOUSE, Salem, Mass. (built 1804) is the work of Salem's great
architect, Samuel McIntire, in a more sophisticated mood. Its proportions are subtle
and satisfying.

The exquisite grace of McIntire's work is well illustrated in this room of the PINGREE HOUSE, Salem. The mantelpiece is ornamented with two delicately carved wheat sheaves.

The formal bedroom of the PINGREE HOUSE has been exquisitely furnished with period pieces and hangings which are in keeping with the subtle refinement of the McIntire mantel.

Two doorways of the PINGREE HOUSE, Salem, give an idea of the skill and restraint of Samuel McIntire who, aside from being an architect, was the most accomplished of Salem's wood carvers.

Samuel McIntire carried this mantel in the PINGREE HOUSE, Salem, about as far as it could go and yet escape the accusation of ornateness.

The PINGREE HOUSE, Salem, affords a glimpse of a formal dining room as it looked in the prosperous days of Salem's shipping and merchant supremacy.

"GRASSMOUNT," Burlington, Vermont (built 1804), is supposed to be the best Georgian house in the state. At present it is used as a women's dormitory in the University of Vermont.

The CLARA BARTON BIRTHPLACE, North Oxford, Mass., is preserved in memory of the great founder of the American Red Cross, who served as a nurse in both the Civil and the Franco-Prussian wars.

The cheerful, well furnished CAPE ANN HISTORICAL HOUSE, built about
1805 in Gloucester, Mass., is filled with ship models, maps, documents and other
graphic momentos of a sailor's hard life.

FORT EDGECOMB, a severe octagonal stronghold overlooking the Sheepscot River in North Edgecomb, Maine, was built in 1808-1809 but never took part in any shooting.

The HISTORICAL BUILDING (built about 1810) in picturesque Hancock, N. H., was for many years a tavern offering food and lodging to travelers along the Milford-Hancock turnpike.

The ANTIQUARIAN HOUSE, Plymouth, Mass. (built 1809), is the characteristic home of a prosperous New England family in the early 19th Century. It is now filled with exhibits of pronounced interest.

The RUGGLES HOUSE, Columbia Falls, Maine (built 1810), is distinguished by superb interior wood carving and by rich doorway and window details outdoors which are unique in this part of New England.

The serene old house which faces the Common in Templeton, Mass., was built about 1810 to serve as the village store and Postoffice. It is now the home of the Narragansett Historical Society.

The SAMUEL FOWLER HOUSE, Danversport, Mass. (built 1810), is a good and perfectly preserved example of a brick dwelling of the early 19th Century. It contains many interesting wall papers.

One of the best rooms in the SAMUEL FOWLER HOUSE contains a delicately reeded mantel surmounted by a finely preserved specimen of the "Roman Chase" wall paper, printed from old blocks.

The impressive CARRINGTON HOUSE, built on a hilltop in Providence, R. I. in 1810-1811, was the home of a successful merchant in the China trade and contains Oriental furniture and objets d'art of great interest.

The SOLOMON ROCKWELL HOUSE, Winsted, Conn., was built in 1813 by a wealthy iron manufacturer. Its unusual porticos, reminiscent of the South, soon gave it the nickname of "Solomon's Temple."

Such details as the barn and cabin of the SOLOMON ROCKWELL HOUSE, Winsted, Conn., are worked out with extraordinary grace and refinement.

The ISAAC DAMON HOUSE in Northampton, Mass. was built in 1812 by one of the outstanding architects of that region, and used as his home. It contains some interesting articles relating to the life of Jenny Lind.

"THE BUTTONWOODS," Haverhill, Mass. (built 1814), was named for a nearby row of trees, planted in 1739. It was once the home of the Saltonstall family, and called "Saltonstall Seat."

The NUTTER HOUSE, Portsmouth, N. H. (built about 1820), was the boyhood home of Thomas Bailey Aldrich, and is furnished as described in his celebrated book, "The Story of a Bad Boy."

The BLACK HOUSE, Ellsworth, Maine, was built early in the 19th Century by Colonel John Black. It contains many furnishings of that period.

The DEACON AMOS BLANCHARD HOUSE, Andover, Mass. (built 1819), contains
the Deacon's account books, showing the current prices for nails, lumber, lime, etc. — as
well as the cost of the New England rum — needed for building at that time.

The EMERSON HOUSE, Concord, Mass. (built 1829), was the home of Ralph Waldo Emerson from 1835 until his death in 1882. The rooms and furniture are virtually unchanged. Emerson's own study has been preserved in the Antiquarian Society, across the street.

The TRASK HOUSE, Manchester, Mass. (built about 1830), has as one of its treasures a model of the frigate *Constitution* made by a seaman of the *Constitution* from a piece of the taffrail of the ship itself.

The WHITTIER HOME, Amesbury, Mass. (built about 1830), claims small architectural distinction, but immense interest as far as the poet is concerned. Whittier lived in Amesbury for more than fifty years, many of them in this house, where he wrote most of his poems, and where his desk and many other relics are still to be seen.

The BLAINE MANSION in Augusta, Maine (built about 1830) was the home of James G. Blaine, who was defeated for the Presidency in 1876. It is now the Executive Mansion.

The SALISBURY HOUSE in Worcester, Mass., designed by Elias Carter and built about 1835, is one of the best examples of the Classical Revival in New England.

All the details of the shoe maker's craft about 1830 are shown in the small LYE
COBBLER'S SHOP, located in the grounds of the Essex Institute in Salem, Mass.

The SPAULDING GRIST MILL in Townsend Harbor, Mass. (built about 1840)
maintains its venerable wooden and wrought iron machinery in good running order.

WIGGIN'S COUNTRY STORE in Northampton, Mass. gives a faithful picture of the picturesque miscellany of goods which used to be sold in a rural Yankee emporium a century or more ago.

The Colonial calm of the CONCORD ANTIQUARIAN SOCIETY'S building (erected in 1929 in Concord, Mass.), hides one of the most exciting exhibits in New England, a collection of early American rooms dating from the earliest pioneer days down through the Victorian period.

Among the fifteen period rooms in the building of the CONCORD ANTIQUARIAN SOCIETY is a superb pine-sheathed room from the 17th Century.

This is the Green Room, dating from the early 18th Century, one of the many rooms which make the CONCORD ANTIQUARIAN SOCIETY house memorable. Emerson's study has been removed intact to this house, and one of Paul Revere's original lanterns is on display.

Open House in New England

Perry Homestead, Wakefield, R.I.

VI

Index